Faith on Fire

Dismantling Structures of Unbelief,
Building Unshakeable Strongholds of Faith

BEN R. PETERS

Faith on Fire

Published by
Kingdom Sending Center
P. O. Box 25
Genoa, IL 60135

www.kingdomsendingcenter.org
ben.peters@kingdomsendingcenter.org

ISBN 13: 978-0-9789884-7-0

Cover image: BigStock Photo #27633632
Cover and book design by *www.ChristianBookDesign.com*

Contents

Chapter One

The Importance of Defeating the Enemies of Faith

In my first year of Bible College, God gave me an insatiable passion to see the blood-bought church of Jesus Christ restored to her original power and glory, as recorded in the early chapters of the book of Acts. I couldn't get enough of that amazing and exciting bit of history. On my knees, in a little piano practice room at Canadian Bible College, I would read the first half of Acts one day and the second half the next. This went on week after week and month after month, often with tears streaming down my face, crying out to God to do it again.

It was just a few years later that a wonderful revival came to our city, Regina, Saskatchewan. It touched thousands with a hunger to walk with God in purity and integrity. There was a reviving of the apathetic church and it was a season of great glory. At the same time, it was not all that my heart had cried out for. I wanted to see the raw power of the jaw-dropping miracles that my heart was crying out for. I had read and heard about them, but I had never really seen them.

But shortly after that Canadian revival had somewhat simmered down, I was invited to accompany an older, seasoned evangelist on his first trip to Argentina. This journey, in the fall of 1973, was the greatest answer that I have ever received to all those prayers. The miracles, signs and wonders were off the charts! Neither Elmer Burnette, the evangelist, Jack Schissler, our host missionary, nor myself had ever seen anything like it!

The most glorious thing about it was that God's presence was so real to everyone from the start of worship until we all went home. People flocked to the front to receive the salvation and healing that Jesus had bought for them. Miraculously, cancer, club feet, crippling arthritis, total deafness (three young men born with no hearing), and many other physical conditions were healed. The result was that the people wanted to know this Jesus who had done all these incredible things. It was very much like the book of Acts, and at least one thousand souls came into the Kingdom of Heaven during the six weeks that we were there. As a confirmation, five new churches rose up, and we were told that after one year only one of them had less than two hundred members. I know that the miracles and conversions in the early church were greater in number, but this was the closest I have been to that kind of power.

Throughout my life, I have been blessed to see many miracles. Some have happened when I prayed, but most of them came when I joined with or witnessed others praying. I have witnessed miracles when Heidi Baker, James Maloney, Bill Johnson, Shawn Bolz, David Herzog, Jeff Jansen, David

Tomberlin and others with great healing ministries prayed for the sick. However, I have never been convinced that what I've personally seen can compare with what was witnessed by the first Apostles in the wonderful book of Acts.

The book of Acts is about a small, but passionate group of followers, led by the apostles who had been empowered by Jesus, and under the direct guidance of the Holy Spirit, produced many miraculous manifestations of the power of the Living God, and changed the face of the world while demonstrating outrageous, agape love.

What was the source of their incredibly fruitful ministry? From many passages of Scripture, I believe it is very clear that the secret to their phenomenal success was a very strong, mature faith, which was anchored and rooted in their passionate love for Jesus and His Kingdom.

Today, decades later, I maintain the long-held conviction that the coming outpouring of God's Spirit will be even more glorious than what we read about in the book of Acts. For that to happen, we must also develop the same mature faith, rooted and grounded in passionate love for Jesus. In that youthful season of my life, God gave me a simple, yet profound, revelation regarding faith and how it grows and produces exceptional results. By the end of my seminary days, based on the simple truth God had revealed to me in the beginning of my second year of college, I was writing my Master's Thesis on the subject of faith. In spite of all the prolific literature (current and ancient), along with so much preaching and teaching on the subject of faith, I have very seldom read or heard this simple truth proclaimed.

I will certainly share at least a portion of this revelation in later chapters, but my primary focus throughout this book will be on the particular aspect of faith that I have been guilty of neglecting. Quite frankly, I failed to understand its importance. This aspect of faith that I had overlooked is not how we build our faith, but rather it is the understanding of how to deal with and defeat the many enemies of the powerful, miracle-working faith that we so desire.

In other words, I want to both learn and then teach how to destroy and eliminate the structures of unbelief that war against our faith. When we have learned how to recognize and tear down these negative structures, we will make much greater progress in building those positive structures of faith, so we can all move the mountains that stand in the way of fulfilling the great commission and expanding the Kingdom of Heaven on the earth.

In the first few chapters of this book, we will expose some of the strongest and most common structures of unbelief. In later chapters, we will discover some keys to tear down these structures and replace them with structures of faith. It is my sincere prayer that these truths will not only change your personal life for the better, but will also help you to bless, increase and prosper the Kingdom of God.

Most Christians wonder why they don't see greater results from their prayers. We know that it is important to have faith, and we try our best to believe, but still we get relatively meager results compared to the early church. Even if we relegate the accomplishments of the early church as unrepeatable history, we get the same unanswered questions. How does our level of power compare to Christians in other seemingly more primitive cultures, where all kinds of miracles, including resurrections from the dead, are being experienced?

Could it be that there are forces arrayed against us to keep us from true and genuine faith? Is it possible that our faith is as unstable as the waves of the sea, as written in the first chapter of James? In that passage, he said this of the person who doubted or hesitated:

For let not that man suppose that he will receive anything from the Lord. (James 1:7)

Until we deal with the issue of doubt and unbelief, we may be bypassing the pathway to pleasing God. We know that without faith it is impossible to please Him. It is also very difficult for our prayers and spiritual gifts to bear fruit, unless we have the faith to believe that He will use those gifts He has given us.

My mentor, Elmer Burnette, used to quote this passage from James, as well as other Scriptures, strongly warning people that doubt and unbelief are serious issues that must be dealt with. In order for faith to flourish like we need it to, we must learn how to overcome our doubts and fears.

Let's take a closer look at the enemy's devices, so we can destroy his works like Jesus did! I'm sure you would love to come closer to His track record when it came to praying for the sick and doing miracles. I know I would sure love to see more people healed when I pray. It doesn't make me happy when, after receiving my prayers, people stay sick or die of cancer, heart disease or any other sickness.

Let me prepare you for what's coming. In the first part of this book, we will discuss the structures that the enemy creates in our souls. The awareness of what has been stacked against us, when it comes to utilizing mountain-moving faith, may be a bit discouraging, but please don't quit reading. The keys to destroying these structures are coming in the later chapters, and these keys will work for everyone who uses them!

These structures of unbelief are not only in our individual souls, but they can also be built into the culture of a nation, people group, denomination, movement or local church group. Influenced by the history of a group, there may be stronger structures of fear, depression or false securities, etc. than in other groups. The same principles for tearing down structures in our soul can be used for tearing down structures in a larger group.

The spiritual leaders of the group have the primary responsibility and authority to tear down these structures, but even those with no official leadership positions can bring breakthrough, if they move into spiritual authority through intimacy with God. No one is "helpless" to bring change to their group. Everyone who stands before God has the opportunity to present his or her supplications before the throne with boldness, and God always hears and answers the prayers and cries of His people.

Chapter Two

Fear

Nothing opposes faith like fear. And guess what! The enemy of your soul knows exactly how to build a structure of fear in your life. The last thing he can tolerate is for you to be a fear-free zone. Should you conquer and delete fear out of your life, you will download terrible fear into his! He has no power to defend his kingdom against a child of God who knows the power of faith and has no fear of anything, including death itself. Remember this awesome verse:

And they overcame him by the blood of the Lamb and by the word of their testimony, and they did not love their lives to the death. (Revelation 12:11)

Notice that THEY DID OVERCOME HIM. Although

the word, "fear" is not mentioned here, they obviously had victory over fear, because "they did not love their lives to the death." The fear of death is one of the strongest fears known to man, but when they overcame that fear, they also overcame the enemy of their souls.

Repeated and reinforced fear soon becomes a structure of fear in your soul. Fear is often prophetic. Job said, *"The thing that I greatly feared has come upon me." (Job 3:25)* When you fear something, which then comes to pass, the brain records the memory for future reference. Whenever you are in a similar situation, your brain tells you that something bad could surely happen to you. The brain is busily connecting the dots and forming internal structures to help you avoid such situations. Recent studies on the brain verify that the brain actually works like this.

There is a positive aspect to this brain activity, as it causes you to be cautious in dangerous situations. The impact on your faith however, is anything but positive, unless you know how to reverse the power of fear and replace it with faith in God. Otherwise, fear will get a stronger and stronger grip on your soul and your ability to believe will be diminished.

There are hundreds of fears or "phobias" known to man. One website lists a total of over 650. Enjoy reading a few good examples below:

- *Ergophobia* – the fear of work.
- *Ecclesiophobia* – the fear of church.
- *Hippopotomonstrosesquipedaliophobia* – Fear of long words.
- *Novercaphobia* – Fear of your step-mother.

ৎ *Omphalophobia* – Fear of belly buttons.

ৎ *Porphyrophobia* – Fear of the color purple.

ৎ *Scolionophobia* – Fear of school.

ৎ *Zemmiphobia* – Fear of the great mole rat.

While these are some of the more humorous examples, there are many serious fears that commonly plague those we would consider "normal" people. They include the fear of speaking in public, the fear of death, the fear of man, the fear of failure, the fear of heights, the fear of abuse, the fear of the dark, the fear of the unknown, the fear of tribulation or torture, the fear of using spiritual gifts (II Tim. 1:6-7), the fear of enemy nations or anti-Christian religions, the fear of war, the fear of aging, the fear of loss of possessions, family members or friends, and the fear of demons or the devil.

There is only one "legal" fear for a Christian – the fear of God. However, I'm sure everyone alive has struggled with some "illegal" fear or another. These "normal" fears are the ones that get us into trouble when we need to have faith in God for miracles.

So where do these fears originate? Many may have begun in the womb. Science is making great headway in discovering how the emotions of the mother affect the emotions of the unborn child. Some of the hormones of the mother, stimulated by her emotions, actually go into the baby through the umbilical cord. Babies can hear what goes on around them. Angry voices, screams and loud music impact their tender emotions. Babies can also see light coming into the womb and have been known to respond to light flashing on and off on the tummy of the mother. You can verify this information by just checking out "emotions in the unborn" on the internet.

So, the chances are that when you made your dramatic debut, you arrived with some invisible baggage, including fear. Soon your senses were taking in more clear evidence that your world was not always safe. Even if your family was highly respected and almost perfect in the eyes of others, you saw the weaknesses of your parents and siblings that were hidden from the public, reinforcing the fears that accompanied your arrival in your delicate soul.

As you grew older you began to attend school, unless your parents made the effort to educate you at home. If you attended a public school or even a private school, or played with other kids on your street, you learned that other kids could be bullies and you could get picked on. Teachers could also embarrass you and then there was always the scary principal, who was there to punish you if you really got in trouble.

But peer fear was soon to become the real slave driver in your life. You would dress a certain way, listen to a certain type of music, hang out at certain places with certain people and speak a certain lingo among your friends. Those friends were just as fearful as you, and everyone was afraid of being mocked or rejected by others, especially by the cool kids. But like most others, you had your good times and survived the peer fear.

As you and your friends responded to the peer fear, the nasty things that happened were motivated by both self-preservation and self-promotion. It was based on fear of not being loved, not being accepted and not being seen as significant. The enemy of your soul was always reinforcing your fears, making sure you felt unworthy, unholy and unloved by God or man.

At a young age, you fell in love for awhile with the coolest person you thought you could convince to like you. Soon either you or your special friend got bored, angry, jealous, or seduced by someone else, and the great breaking-up experience had begun. The pain was serious, and once it had happened, you were filled with fear that the next relationship would end in a similar way. It probably did, and the experience reinforced your basic notions that you were not very attractive, loveable or fun to be with.

Even though you may have had a family that properly loved you, you needed people outside the family, whom you felt would not be prejudiced, to accept and honor you, so that you could feel you truly had value and worth. Sadly, there were not too many who were there to help you. Most of your peers were just as insecure and fearful as you were, and they were in no condition to make you feel secure without expecting something in return. Sadly, you may have been one who was willing to give your selfish friend something in return for his or her help, and you ended up feeling guilty or dirty instead of more secure.

Every time your fears were reinforced by another disappointment or painful experience, the enemy was able to build a structure of fear. No matter what the fear was, the foundation of the fear was this:

> *Bad things will likely happen to me. God and others have let me down before and they will probably let me down again. I cannot trust God or my friends, and I cannot believe their promises.*

Fast forward now to the present day when you are praying for someone dying of cancer. You want to have real faith because you know that God responds to faith according to Scripture. You pray for a miracle, but the structure or stronghold of fear has never been dismantled and removed from your life. You try to believe, but you are reminded of the last person with cancer who died when you prayed. How can you know this one will not end up with the same result? The enemy of faith will speak from within the structure of fear, which he has been stealthily building in your soul over the years. He will remind you of all your past failures and how unfaithful God has been to you, in spite of all that you have done for Him.

From within this structure of fear, the enemy can hijack your faith and prevent it from producing results. God is very merciful to answer many of our prayers, in spite of our doubts and fears, but He longs for us to learn how to remove the structures of unbelief, so that we can truly walk in His faith.

I want to make it clear that this subject is important to me. We have also prayed for many terminally ill people, especially cancer patients, and our hearts have been broken watching so many of them leaving this world before their time, several of them being mothers with children still to be raised. You wish you could explain things better or give greater understanding when you have to repeatedly answer the question, "Why didn't they get healed?" In most cases, people are too filled with grief and emotional turmoil to really want a theological answer. They need more comfort than answers, but there comes a time when we all need to search for God's answers, if we want to see better results than we are seeing today.

Fear is a powerful, negative force, and it is probably the most frequently used tactic by the enemy of your faith. If you learn to conquer fear, you are well on your way to destroying the structures of unbelief in your life and building powerful structures of faith. As we mentioned earlier, the keys to removing these structures are coming later in the book. But as we shall quickly see, there are many other structures of unbelief that the enemy can use to keep you from exercising the awesome power of faith.

Chapter Three

Science, Secular Education and Unbiblical Church Teachings

When you began attending formal school, the enemy of your faith had a strategy to establish another structure of unbelief. Little by little, you were taught to shed your childlike faith in a Creator and supernatural happenings and learn to think with pure reason and logic. The scientific method would become the god that you worshipped, and you would discard all the ancient fairy tales and fables you had been taught.

After all, you would eventually realize that Santa Claus and the Easter bunny were not real. When you grow up you don't need the fairy tales anymore. Your religion might be tolerated, but there could be no such thing as miracles, because only primitive people, who did not understand science, were that superstitious. Science would eventually explain everything in the universe and replace all religious beliefs.

If you attended college or university, the intellectual pride may have gotten so thick you could cut it with a knife. The main strategy used by professors in my day to discredit anything religious or supernatural was to just mock it. Believers were made to feel that they are a small and ignorant minority, still living in the dark ages. Everyone was superstitious in those ancient times, as they did not have modern science to explain things they could not understand. And if you believe in supernatural events, such as the virgin birth, the resurrection of Jesus or the miracles that He performed, you are just a left-over dinosaur.

How does this hellish strategy affect us who do believe in a supernatural God and have even experienced miracles in the past? Sadly, the impact may be subtle, but it is certainly real and effective. The structure of science and education joins forces with the structure of fear, and it helps to barricade the pathway to powerful faith. Knowing that many intelligent people will think we are weird and ignorant if we believe in miracles, we may be timid about proclaiming or declaring our faith. We may even question whether we have enough assurance to stick our neck out.

This hesitation could very possibly be just enough to rob us of the faith that we are nurturing in our heart and soul. As James says,

> *But let him ask in faith, with no doubting, for he who doubts is like a wave of the sea driven and tossed by the wind. For let not that man suppose that he will receive anything from the Lord; he is a double-minded man, unstable in all his ways. (James 1:6-8)*

That's pretty strong! Could hesitating because of fear of people's opinion be equivalent to doubting God's promises? Could this then cause of our limited results when praying for miracles? Could it be that the old saying is true: "He who hesitates is lost"?

I have written in previous books about the planned and effective takeover of our education system by secular humanists. This takeover was led by Horace Mann, who is called the "Father of American Education" and John Dewey, who picked up where Mann left off in the 1900's. Most Christians are still unaware of the conspiracy to destroy the Christian faith of future generations through secular humanistic education. At one time, about 80% of the top teachers in the nation were taught by the professors of Colombia University, under John Dewey. These teachers were taught to make their desks the pulpit of a new religion – secular humanism. This religion, as enunciated in the Humanist Manifesto I, taught that man is alone and determines his own future. Dewey declared that no deity will save us; rather, we must save ourselves.

This teaching has obviously had devastating results in America, Europe and many other nations of the world. The atheistic worldview of science, combined with the religion of secular humanism, has robbed our children and youth of the belief in the very existence of God, let alone the belief in His love and power to do miracles for us and through us for His Kingdom.

But for those of us who do believe that God is alive and well and still wants to show us His power and glory, we must recognize the structures of unbelief that have been built in our own heart and soul. In later chapters, we will give specific instructions and keys to destroying every structure that the enemy has been able to build in our lives.

Unbiblical Church Doctrines

If it wasn't bad enough to have our faith attacked by our secular educators, a huge segment of western Christianity has also had their faith attacked by church leaders, in whom the common people have often put their trust. The devastating doctrine of Cessationism has crippled the faith of scores of millions of Christians. They were told that the miracles in the Bible were true, but that God no longer did miracles today. Now that we have the complete Bible, they tell us, we don't need the miracles any more. As illogical and unbiblical as this doctrine is, it has been accepted by church leaders and theologians as an excuse for the pathetically powerless and faithless church. If God doesn't do miracles anymore, then we don't have to feel bad about our own weak faith when people are not healed like they were in Bible times.

Thus we can justify our religious, but powerless style of Christianity, and we don't have to seek God's face or fast and pray for a greater manifestation of His power and glory. This is a very convenient doctrine for theologians, based on extremely flawed exegesis of two or three passages in Scripture, but motivated by a desire to justify their religious traditions and lack of faith.

The tragedy of it all is that the faith of multitudes of evangelical "believers" is severely crippled, and the structures of unbelief are built into their lives from both outside and inside the church. These false teachings, even though one turns away from them, can still subconsciously weaken the faith of someone who is trying to believe in God, while remaining a part of that unbelief structure built in us by those seemingly wise and educated people in their lives.

To those whose religious background included this doctrine of unbelief, I suggest that you do as suggested in Leviticus 26. Confess your own sins of unbelief and the sins of your spiritual fathers, who probably taught this doctrine in ignorance, having been taught it themselves by their own spiritual fathers. I deal with this topic in greater detail in my book, *Catching Up to the Third World.* Especially read the chapter entitled, "The Leviticus Key."

Chapter Four

Substitute Sources of Security

Modern False Gods

The first commandment made it very clear that God is a jealous God and does not take it lightly when we replace Him with other "gods" or sources of security. But in our western world, we have a full shelf of idols and well-cared-for shrines where we pay our faithful homage and give of our material substance. In outlining some of our favorite western idols, I knowingly take the risk of sounding political, but that does not concern me as much as taking the risk of leaving God's people uninformed and deceived by the enemy of our faith.

Jonah 2:8 declares: Those who cling to, preserve, protect or guard, vain or deceitful idols, forsake or relinquish their own mercy (the mercy that God would give to them). (This is my own loose translation after studying the word meanings in the Hebrew text.)

False Gods Have the Power to Destroy Us

The first major point to be made in this chapter is that whatever we look to for security, in place of our trust in God, will eventually turn on us and destroy us.

False Gods Distract Us from the One True God

The second major point is that with so many forms of protection and security available to us (none of them evil in or of themselves), we have less need and opportunity to exercise our faith in God. It's nice not to have any worries, but it's tragic that when our other "gods" can't save us, we barely know how to approach our "last resort", which is our omnipotent God, our Creator and the creator of everything visible and invisible.

As we examine each of the following common sources of security in the western world, we will see how our trust has shifted little by little from the one true God to our substitute "gods". This has resulted in a creeping deterioration of our faith. But please don't despair! We don't have to get rid of all the benefits of western life – we only have to take the idols down from their exalted places and put God in the "High Place" of our hearts and minds. We must become aware of these deceitful idols and acknowledge that we have become much too dependent on them, with too little dependence on God.

David was known as a man after God's own heart, and he

repeatedly wrote that God was His only source. Read carefully the following excerpt:

> *Truly my soul silently waits for God; From Him comes my salvation. He is my defense, I shall not be greatly moved. My soul, wait silently for God alone, for my expectation is from Him. **He only** is my rock and my salvation; He is my defense; I shall not be moved. In God is my salvation and my glory; the rock of my strength, and my refuge is in God. Trust in Him at all times, you people; pour out your heart before Him; God is a refuge for us. (Psalms 62:1-2, 5-8)*

IMPORTANT DISCLAIMER: *I don't desire to criticize or judge anyone in any institution, profession or occupation mentioned in the material following. Each one has a legitimate place in society. There are many wonderful people doing their best to help people in their field of expertise. I am only pointing out the effects of our putting undue trust in these entities and replacing God as our source of security and provision.*

Western Society's Sources of Security

1. Government

We will begin with one of the largest idols on the shelf – Government. Depending on what country you live in, you expect various levels of government to take care of a multitude of needs for you. In America, most citizens can rely on the government to provide the following means of safety and security:

1. Social Security – income for retirement
2. Medicare – medical insurance coverage in old age
3. Welfare, food stamps, unemployment benefits – when we need them
4. Military – to protect from foreign powers
5. Police – to protect from local criminals
6. Fire Department – in case of fire
7. 911 – a number to call in an emergency

As everyone knows, governments in democratic societies tend to expand and grow to handle the increased services and benefits desired by their citizens. Of course, they also have to raise more taxes and charge higher fees to pay for those benefits. More and more people end up either working for the government or being supported by the government through entitlement programs.

The politicians like to offer more benefits to those who elected them, because that seems like the easiest way to get reelected. They love giving away other people's money and getting rewarded for it. At the same time as they are giving away taxpayer money, they can vote themselves pay increases, lucrative pension plans and healthcare benefits. No wonder they work so hard to get elected! When they have millions of taxpayers to draw from, the tax increases can be very small and almost unnoticeable for a while. But little by little and dollar by dollar, they raise our taxes and fees until enough people realize they are giving up a huge part of their income and rise up to challenge the system.

Aside from the long-term economic destruction resulting from the above scenario, the main point I wish to emphasize is that the government has replaced the need for God as the ultimate source for many people. This dependence on an earthly "god", takes a big bite out of our capacity to believe in God, because it takes away some of our need to exercise our faith in God in times of need.

It also needs to be made clear that our dependence on a false "god" causes us to suffer greatly. We see the fruit of it in the economic crises happening all over the world, especially in nations like Greece and Spain, where those governments have provided the most services to their people. Many countries have resorted to borrowing heavily until their ability to pay their debts has been destroyed by their extravagant spending.

The idol has cruelly bitten those who worship it.

2. Medical Science

The second source of security we have in the western world is medical science. This includes our doctors and medical researchers who seek to cure diseases. The incredible advances in medical science have offered hope to multiplied millions of people who have been afflicted with diseases which formerly had no known cure.

Today, many of these diseases have been virtually eliminated from society while others, like leprosy, are confined to a few remote places on the earth. Medical science has developed pain killers, sleep aids, antibiotics, organ transplants, noninvasive surgical procedures, testing and scanning procedures, such as EKG's, and so much more. Life expectancy has improved, and we have all greatly benefited from these scientific advances.

However, even medical science has its limitations. Like the woman we read about in Luke 8:43, who had spent all her livelihood on physicians and could not be cured, many people come to the end of their resources and those of their earthly doctors. If the Great Physician does not perform a miracle for them, they face the certainty of an untimely death. By the time they reach this point, they have had so much experience with medical science, and so little experience exercising their faith, that their personal faith for healing is usually very weak.

While the benefits of medical scientific advances are huge and obvious, let's take a peek at the specific problems accompanying them. We can thank God for the blessings, but we must be aware of the associated dangers.

First of all, and most importantly, is the way we are taught to put our absolute faith and trust in our doctors. Most drug commercials are accompanied by a statement saying that only your doctor knows for sure what you should use in your situation. We are warned frequently not to diagnose ourselves, but to follow the advice of our doctors.

My wife worked many years in hospitals as an operating room technician, and she observed how many of the surgeons acted like little "gods" and demanded respect and almost worship. Because the lives of so many people were in their hands, they tended to feel superior to normal human beings. They also were paid accordingly; with wealth comes power and often arrogance. To be fair, they also had huge pressures and responsibilities and the "buck" stopped with them.

Obviously, we can easily see how natural it is to replace our Almighty God, the Great Physician, with a human doctor that we can see and talk to, when it comes to our physical health. We only have one body and one life, and we hate being sick and in pain. We want relief as quickly as possible, and the doctor usually has the answers. We may ask God first, but with little history of answers to such prayers, we quickly turn our faith to the doctor we can see.

Another potential problem with our current system of healthcare is that we may be deprived of some of the more natural treatments that God gave us. The medical establishment frequently warns us against the use of alternative medicine. For example, the American Medical Association fought against the acceptance of chiropractors for some time, and many medical doctors frequently mocked the "health nut" folk for thinking food and diet could cure or prevent diseases. They succeeded in outlawing certain treatments for cancer, forcing people with no other hope to go to Mexico or other countries, where they could try those treatments.

Some medical practitioners were arrested for giving people vitamin shots for certain conditions. There were many testimonials of cures, but the medical establishment had too much to lose to allow such inexpensive treatments.

The huge amount of money involved in our current medical system makes it an easy target for abuse and corruption. There are many horror stories out there of inventors of cures who have been taken out abruptly and mysteriously with untimely accidents before their cures could go public. Many people believe that there are already many working cures for diseases like cancer, but they would so devastate the established multibillion dollar health industry that they have been suppressed. Only when they can produce an expensive drug to cure these diseases, will they be accepted by the medical establishment.

We have no way of knowing how much of this is happening or how many people have died due to cure suppression, but I believe it is a significant number. I have personally heard some of these stories, and I trust those who related them to me.

Another obvious problem with our healthcare system is that prices have skyrocketed far beyond the rate of inflation. This has happened for a number of reasons, one of which will be looked at in the next segment. The overriding reason is, of course, the desire for personal wealth, which we all have, but it is more attainable by those who have the exclusive knowledge and skills to keep us alive and free from pain, when we would otherwise lose our lives or wellbeing.

These men and women certainly paid a hefty price in time and money when they put themselves through medical school, and they deserve a financial reward for their important work. However, the system is such that, with the blessing of their exclusive medical associations, they can easily use their skills as an opportunity to greatly increase their wealth. Of course, I'm not just speaking of physicians, but also those who make and sell hospital and research equipment, those who administrate and virtually everyone involved in the healthcare process.

In addition to what we have just discussed, there is another cause for skyrocketing prices. It is the next false god that we are going to look at.

3. Insurance: Home, Auto, Health, Life, Accidental Death, etc.

Insurance is such a wonderful idea. What sounds more "Christian" than a plan to share one another's burdens? And, in fact, it has been a huge blessing to millions of people who would have lost everything without it.

So why are we about to look at this institution in a negative light? The reason is that while it has done much good and sounds really "Christian", we have been deceived into allowing insurance to become the "god" that saves us from every possible danger. David referred to God as his "Rock", but today we have Prudential – the Rock of Gibraltar – as the rock on which we can stand for protection.

I want to also show you how this "god" in our society has become more of a terrorist than a blessing. The idol has bitten us and the bite could be fatal.

Insurance of various kinds have been with us for some time. Benjamin Franklin was involved in promoting fire insurance in the early days of nationhood. In 1752, he helped establish a fire insurance company in Philadelphia, and in 1759, he added a life insurance company, originally for Presbyterian ministers. For some time, insurance companies played a very helpful role. For instance, the fire insurance companies refused to insure those who built houses that were considered fire traps. This led to better building construction standards, which reduced house fires and tragic deaths. Additionally, if their husbands had purchased life insurance, widows were able to take better care of themselves.

However, before insurance was widespread, most people depended upon family, friends and neighbors, as well as their faith in God, to care for them in times of emergency. Families were closely knit and the majority of early Americans had a local church and community that cared about them individually. They formed volunteer fire departments and pitched in to rebuild a house or barn that had burned to the ground. Doctors and nurses knew their patients more intimately, and they had compassion on those going through financial hardship and were unable to pay them.

If someone in the community died, the extended family, church and community would pitch in to support the widows or orphans for however long was needed. There was little need for auto insurance when you drove a horse-drawn carriage, and there was much less crime and little need for theft insurance. Most people never locked their doors and neighbors watched out for one another.

However, that scenario is gone forever or at least until the Millennium. We live in a fast-paced society, where few people know, or trust, their closest neighbors. Families are scattered, living in different parts of the country, and fewer people attend a local church. Many that do attend church are part of huge mega-churches and have little relationship with other members during the week, even though the churches make an effort to alleviate that problem with small group meetings.

We have become a nation of individuals who want more and more independence from one another. We want to be able to take care of ourselves without ever asking for help or having to give help to others. We are more comfortable receiving help from the government, because government handouts don't require us to beg from people we know. Since it is a very impersonal interaction, we don't feel any obligation to return the favor or even say thank you. It's not a person, it's the government, and we feel entitled to the benefit because we have paid some taxes along the way.

Insurance policies fit perfectly into our preferred way of life today. If we can insure our health, our vehicles, our homes, our lives and all our possessions, we are given a sense of security and independence from everyone, including our family, friends, neighbors, church and God, Himself.

Thus, insurance has a powerful appeal to our human nature in today's society. It is the "god" we can count on in almost any crisis. It is real, tangible and always there for us. We would love to just trust in God and save the hassle and expense of insurance, but God seems to not hear us at times. We don't know if He will provide for our emergencies, so insurance is such a great thing to have.

Let's take a look at some of the consequences of putting our trust in this "idol".

My first memory of insurance was the accident insurance package that came to us through the public school I attended, Connaught School, in North Battleford, Saskatchewan. For $3.00, they would insure the family against accidents. My parents decided to purchase this insurance, and sure enough, I had an accident playing hockey and had two front teeth broken. The dentist would have charged the enormous sum of $70.00 for the work and the partial to replace the two teeth, but it was free for us. Our family rejoiced at this provision of God. $70.00 was more than a week's wages for my dad at the time, and there was no way they could have afforded it.

But that was then – about fifty-some years ago. Today, insurance fees have exceeded what anyone would have predicted. People consider insurance a complete necessity, while government tries to force us to get more and more of it. The profit motive – a basically positive thing in the mix of our western society – has attracted the formation of countless insurance companies, insuring everything imaginable to get in on the opportunity to make some good money from people who demand more and more security.

If you watch TV, especially the news channels that I watch, you won't get through an evening without at least a half dozen insurance commercials from various competing companies. Those commercials aren't cheap. Where do they get the money for their ads? That's right – they pay for them with your premium dollars. And you thought your premiums went to pay for emergencies and accidents, etc.

Insurance companies advertise because there is a lot more money to be made, and they want to get a larger share of the pie. Not only do insurance companies spend your premium dollars on these ads, but they also build huge office buildings, hire thousands of employees, lobby governments, sponsor (at great expense) huge events and put their names on sports stadiums, such as Safeco Field in Seattle. Where do they get the millions of dollars for these expenses? Again, the answer is from your insurance premiums. Is it any wonder those premiums are so high?

But that's not all…it gets much worse. Enter the world of lawyers and lawsuits. Our desire for tangible security didn't go unnoticed by this group of opportunists. Usually working on a commission basis, lawyers seek for the largest possible settlement for their clients when suing someone for damages.

The extremely important factor is that they are not suing a doctor, a hospital, a driver, an arsonist, etc. They are suing an insurance company, and they know that the insurance company has what they call "deep pockets." If they were suing the individual, they know they could only get a small amount of money. The judge would not allow the lawsuit to unreasonably devastate an unfortunate individual who accidentally caused some type of personal or property damage.

But the multi-billion dollar insurance industry is a lot like the government. It not only has deep pockets, but it can create more resources. The government does it with increased taxes and printing new money. The insurance companies can do it through raising their fees. Since people are required to buy many types of insurance, and those they are not required to purchase they desperately want, insurance companies can and do get away with it.

Let's check out what happens in the medical field. Today, doctors can be sued for huge amounts of money, because they deal with life and death issues all the time. They have to spend a lot of money on insurance because of these huge lawsuits. I recently interviewed a doctor who shared the fact that some doctors pay as much as $150,000 per year on insurance premiums.

OBGYN's need to have coverage for deliveries they performed until the child is eighteen years old. In other words, if some expert insists that the seventeen-year-olds problem stems from some malpractice when the baby was born, the doctor can be sued.

An anesthesiologist told me that he has to pay a $50,000 premium when he retires, in case someone sues him years later. So, when he retires, he not only loses his working income, but he has to save up to pay the $50,000 premium. Who is actually paying those huge expenses to the doctor and the hospital you go to in your time of need? Yes, it is you, the patient. Even if your insurance company pays 100% of your medical costs, your premiums are paying for those inflated medical costs that the insurance company is paying for.

A doctor also told me that most lawsuits will not be fought in court. To fight the lawsuit requires hours or even days off work and the cost of an attorney. Unless the amount is huge, they choose to just settle out of court. Attorneys know just how much to sue for, knowing they will win the case without a fight. And so, the inflationary spiral keeps going and going and going…

Let's follow the money trail. The following is a general scenario – not one which is always followed each step of the way. It will however, average out this way:

- ❧ I want security, so I pay for health insurance, or any other type of insurance.
- ❧ I have a medical emergency.
- ❧ The doctor and hospital and lab charge me an enormous amount of money.
- ❧ My insurance company pays most of the bill – say 80%.
- ❧ I still end up with a substantial payment to the healthcare professionals.
- ❧ My rates go up because the insurance company needs to recover its cost.
- ❧ Someone else with the same insurance sues my doctor and hospital.
- ❧ The insurance company pays a huge lawsuit settlement.
- ❧ The insurance company raises the premium of the doctor and hospital.
- ❧ They also raise my premiums, because their costs are rising.
- ❧ The doctor and hospital raise their fees for service because their costs are up.
- ❧ My next visit to the doctor or hospital will cost me more than the first time.
- ❧ My fees, which are already higher, will go up again.

Today, insurance fees take a huge bite out of the average worker's income. The beneficiaries are primarily the lawyers and insurance companies. But with so much money passing through so many hands, others are also taking their cut. After all, the insurance companies have lots of money, don't they?

Yes, insurance companies have a lot of money going through their hands, but don't forget where that money comes from. It comes from people in a society who want to be self-sufficient and don't need anyone to help them. We are making them wealthy! We are paying for their cute ads. We are paying for their skyscrapers. We are paying the salaries of thousands of marketing experts. And we are going broke, as families and as nations.

Once again, the idol has turned on us and we are reeling under the poison of its bite. Where does it end and what is the solution to this dilemma? We will talk about that in a later chapter. Please stay with us for some answers.

4. Money and Investments: IRA's, Stocks, Bonds, Gold, Silver, Real Estate, etc.

If riches increase, do not set your heart on them. (Psalm 62:10b)

Another potential idol is trust in wealth – both small and great. David warned us not to put our trust in riches. Jesus also warned against using wealth as a form of security, when He told the story of the rich man and Lazarus. Paul told Timothy that the love of money was a root of all kinds of suffering and evil things happening. It is not "the" root as wrongly translated by the King James Version. It is just one source of much of the suffering in our world.

Wealth is another one of those entities that can be used for good or evil. It can be a tremendous blessing, but it can also cause people to turn their hearts away from God. When you have money, you know that you have a certain amount of power. When you wield a certain amount power, your perception of and need for God diminishes. When you don't feel a need for God, your faith is not stimulated.

As Bill Johnson says, "The trouble we go through in life is to prepare us to survive the blessings that are coming." Prosperity is a more difficult test to pass than poverty or difficult circumstances. But what a blessing we can be if we have the right heart and wealth at the same time!

The money "idol" has come back to haunt us and bite us in many ways. People who invest for security purposes often find their investments have disintegrated or seriously declined in value. There is always fear of a stock market crash, a recession or depression. Even gold and silver have been up and down like a yoyo. In the past decade or so, many retirement packages were reduced to ashes when companies, like Enron, in which they were heavily invested, went bankrupt overnight. Other times, inflation has come like a thief to steal the value of our money.

Even real estate cannot be depended upon. The house we purchased eight years ago is now worth far less than the purchase price. Millions of homes in America are under water financially and commercial real estate is suffering as well. Aggressive commercial development projects have been left uncompleted in our neighborhood, and the new home construction that was booming is down to a tiny trickle.

Our security cannot rest in our financial resources. It can only rest in God. He must be our true Source.

5. Education: Preschool – Post Graduate

Educators often like to impart the impression that knowledge is the answer to all of our problems. It is true that the lack of knowledge is a destructive thing, according to Scripture. But knowledge without wisdom can also be destructive, in that knowledge puffs a person up, making him proud, and pride goes before destruction and a haughty spirit before a fall. (Proverbs 16:18)

Many parents, including Christian parents, see education as the most important thing to give their children. They drill it into them that if they don't get good grades in school, they won't be able to get into a good university, and then they won't get a good job and make a comfortable living. The parents save for years for the coming college expenses and send them to the best schools they can afford. They believe that this is the formula for success. Often the parents have been hindered by their own lack of education and want their kids to do better. Others have seen the financial and social rewards of their own higher education and want their kids to have at least the same status in life that they have enjoyed.

As we have mentioned in a previous chapter, this idol of education can also turn on us and bite us. How many young Christians have been brainwashed to accept the philosophies of man, including evolution, free sex, abortion, homosexuality and radical political points of view because of the education system that their parents paid for? No one knows the number of wayward young people, but each one is a tragedy, and often totally unnecessary.

As parents, we need to seek the Lord before we send our children to any school, from Kindergarten to University. What is our priority? Is it economic status, or is it the perfect will of God? It is true that God wants Christians to go to the top of every mountain, including medicine, law, sports and other high paying professions. However, we can only be truly successful for the Kingdom of God if we have the right motive for getting to the top of those mountains. Are we seeking the Kingdom of God first, or our own prosperity? The very same value system that we endorse by the way we live will probably be unconsciously adopted by our children.

Our own children knew that their walk with God was more important to us than having a good career. Today, all five are serving God. All have been to Bible College and the oldest four are married to wonderful Christian partners. They bring great joy to us, as we interact with them and our ten amazing grandchildren.

All five children have had a Christian education. So far, none of them have attended any secular school, although I have no problem with them going to a secular college, if that is where God is sending them. God sent me to a university while in a seminary program. My goal was preparation for ministry, not personal wealth, and God kept me from the many dangers and temptations available in any university.

Meanwhile, we've prayed with many parents whose children have wandered far from God, while pursuing the career that their parents desired for them. The parents only wanted the best for their children, but perhaps they had some wrong values and the god of education became the idol that turned on its worshippers and broke their hearts.

6. Friends, Family and Allies: Those with influence, wealth or political power

Once again, I need to make it perfectly clear that friends, family and allies can be a tremendous blessing from God. But just like money, government, education, insurance and medical science, we can become more dependent upon them than on God. The sad result is that we seldom exercise our faith, and then when we really need it, we find our faith very weak and ineffective.

Some people find security in making lots of friends, especially those with a lot of wealth or power. They can always find a friend who knows the person that can help them. They have the ability to get people to like them. They serve people in ways that subtly obligate them to return a favor when it's needed.

We may put our trust in a great lawyer or politician. We may put our trust in our accountant or even our pastor or other spiritual leader. Whenever we elevate a human being to that place of honor that belongs only to Jesus, we have created an idol that won't be able to help us in our time of need.

So many religious leaders, political leaders and professional people have let us down in the past. For instance, how many people have served, loved and given sacrificially to Christian leaders whom they admired, and suddenly their evil secrets were exposed by the media. Many Christians have been devastated by the failures of their pastors or favorite TV preacher, because they put their trust and focus in a man or woman, rather than becoming intimate with Jesus themselves.

Once again, to get back to the main point – we see that putting our trust in people can not only end up hurting us directly, but putting our trust in people tends to weaken our trust in God. As long as we have people meeting our every physical, social, emotional and financial need, we don't really need God all that much and we spend little time seeking Him and exercising our precious faith.

7. Unions

Unions are just one more example of the false gods that we depend upon for our prosperity and security. But like all the rest of them, we find that the entity we trust to be for us turns around to bite or sting us. While unions appeared to be for the little guy against the rich and ruthless, in the end we find that many unions bosses also become the rich and ruthless themselves, and spend the compulsory union dues on political power for their own selfish purposes. Whether the union workers agree with the union's political views or not, their union dues support candidates chosen by the union bosses.

In public employee unions, the employer is the government, paying with taxpayer dollars. Using political influence, these unions convince our government representatives to give them whatever they want. The representatives are not like bosses using their own money to pay benefits, retirements, etc., so there is no motivation to limit these benefits. They would rather retain favor with the unions, so they are motivated to give them more than the country, state, county or city can afford.

As we have seen recently, the unions, which were supposed to be a blessing to the employees, have put state governments, like California, on the verge of bankruptcy. The state can't afford the promised retirements and other entitlement benefits. Most American states, where joining a union is required, are deep in debt and declining in population because the jobs have disappeared. On the contrary, in the right to work states, like Texas, they are prospering and growing.

People come because jobs are available, and companies gravitate to them because their taxes are lower. On the other hand, the taxes in other states have to increase to cover the burden of benefits and pensions that were promised to people over the years. Politicians made promises they knew they couldn't keep, but they succeeded in getting reelected by giving the unions what they asked for.

Today, at least in America, unions are in a period of decline, and people no longer see them as the blessing they once seemed to be. Ultimately, every "god" we put our trust in will let us down, and we will see the foolishness of our ways. So often, when the light finally dawns on us, it's much too late to escape some level of loss.

8. Entertainment: The Perpetual Pacifier

While entertainment may not meet any material needs in our lives, it does function as a pacifier or a distraction, so we don't spend as much time worrying about other situations. Like booze to an alcoholic, entertainment of all kinds can keep us from thinking about our nagging fears and responsibilities.

Entertainers, from movie stars to sports stars, from comedians to musicians and dancers, can all be idolized and given undue emotional attention. With all the modern technology, entertainment is so much more available than ever before, and those of us in the western world spend huge amounts of time listening to, watching and emulating our favorite entertainers.

Like preachers who fall into sin and disrepute, many entertainers and sports stars have left their fans disillusioned when they run into trouble with the law or commit suicide. Some of the greatest athletes, in different sports, have faced charges for using steroids or other performance enhancing drugs. It is extremely disillusioning to young idealistic fans when their heroes end up in prison or even dead at their own hands.

As parents, we have the responsibility to teach our children not to make idols out of human beings, no matter how talented and "cool" they seem to be. We can teach them to enjoy the gifting that God has given men and women, but to always make Jesus their true hero. Jesus already has a perfect track record, and He is the only one who deserves our worship.

I'd like to sum up this chapter with two other relevant Scriptures.

> *Then your altars shall be desolate, your incense altars shall be broken, and I will cast down your slain men before your idols. And I will lay the corpses of the children of Israel before their idols and I will scatter your bones all around your altars. (Ezekiel 6:4-5)*

When Israel was worshipping idols, God warned them that their idols would not save them. He also told them that their idols and altars would be destroyed, those who worshipped them would die, and their bodies and bones would be scattered around the altars of their false gods.

Idolatry always brings some form of death to the idol worshipper. The idols prove to be weak and powerless to help those who depend upon them. They will not prosper, or as Jonah put it, "Those who look to their idols forsake their own mercy."

Their sorrows shall be multiplied, who hasten after another god. (Ps. 16:4)

Both individuals and nations have proven this truth many times. We also know that God's blessing makes us rich and adds no sorrow with it. (Proverbs 10:22) Though God asks us to lay everything on the altar, which to some seems like a really painful sacrifice, the end result is His blessing, which makes us rich, and no sorrow accompanies that wonderful blessing. In contrast, all the "gods" that promise us success and happiness leave us with a curse and plenty of sorrow, instead of the great goodies they promised us at the beginning.

Summing Up Structures of Unbelief

As described to this point, the western world has a lot of hindrances to miracle-working faith. It's like the very air we breathe is impregnated with anti-faith particulates. We inhale natural thinking molecules that provide no life for the faith process. The actual air we breathe may be full of oxygen, but the spiritual atmosphere we breathe is more like a high concentration of carbon dioxide, as far as our faith is concerned. Our environment is polluted and poisonous to our spiritual life of faith.

What is the antidote and how can our circumstances be changed, so that our faith gets the oxygen it needs? It's time to begin addressing the solution – God's answer to the dilemma. God has not left us helpless and His answers, which we will explore, will not only give us hope, but they will trigger a passion in us to not only change our environment but that of those we dearly love.

Chapter Five

Understanding the Simplicity of Faith

If we want to dismantle and destroy structures of unbelief in our life, it is important that we understand the basic essence of faith. What is amazing to me is that with all the teaching on the subject over the past half-century and beyond, very few people seem to understand what faith really is and how to make it grow in their lives.

The fact is that faith is such an easy and simple concept to understand that we miss it entirely. It is thought of as a great and mysterious phenomenon that we must reach for by convincing our mind to agree with God's word, when we need something from God. So Christians everywhere are doing mental gymnastics, trying to convince their minds that they believe, when their hearts are actually in a place of doubt and fear.

My favorite illustration of this fact comes from my childhood.

When my brother, Dave, was about eight years old or younger, he really wanted a bicycle. It wasn't a priority in our very tight family budget, but we heard about a bicycle giveaway on the local radio station. There was a children's program, which we often listened to after school, and they were doing a drawing for a brand new bicycle.

Dave had either been reading the Bible for himself, or he had been listening to preaching regarding the promises of Jesus that declared whatever we ask, if we believe, we will receive it. He was an adventurous young man and willing to try almost anything once, so he decided to put this Bible verse to the test. He entered the contest and began to tell his family and close friends that he was going to win that bicycle. He did everything he could think of to prove he had faith, including visualizing where he was going to park it.

When the Saturday morning program was ready to be aired in our little city, we were all positioned around the radio to hear the announcer tell the whole world that David Peters had won the coveted bicycle. Finally, as a finale to the program, they picked the winning entry. They reached into the bucket and pulled out one name. We listened with expectancy. Would this experiment prove successful? Would Dave's faith produce the desired result, or would he be disappointed or disillusioned?

The announcer read the name. For some reason, it sounded nothing like David Peters, and we had to cancel our trip to the radio station to pick up the prize of his faith. As far as I can remember, it wasn't too devastating to Dave, although he reminisces that he did give it some serious thought, trying to figure out what went wrong.

Dave has been living a great life as a missionary to Colombia,

Brazil and Mexico, serving Jesus as a Christian and Missionary Alliance missionary and visiting many other countries to encourage pastors and believers. Overall, when it came to his faith experiment, I believe he simply chalked it up as a "nothing ventured, nothing gained" adventure. He had nothing to lose, and if it had worked, he would have had a brand new bicycle.

This simple story, however, clearly illustrates my point. Obviously, there was some missing ingredient in my brother's childlike faith. He made every effort to convince his mind that he believed, but he never succeeded in producing true faith. Millions of Christians have experienced the same disappointing results, doing everything they know of, trying to qualify for that "whatsoever you ask will be given you" reward.

Faith is Simple But Not as Easy as We Would Like it to Be

Sometimes our biggest problem is that we separate the spiritual realm from the natural realm, and we don't realize that the natural was given to us to help us understand the spiritual. Jesus always used natural things to illustrate Kingdom truths. He even compared both faith and the Kingdom of Heaven to a mustard seed. He compared the harvest of souls to the natural harvest. He compared the treasures of Heaven to natural treasures on earth. He compared Himself to a shepherd and us to sheep.

To understand faith in God, you simply take a closer look at the natural faith we have in people. The same principles totally apply. Let's keep it very simple.

Simple Faith Principle

WE TRUST OR BELIEVE IN TRUSTWORTHY PEO-PLE THAT WE HAVE GOTTEN TO KNOW. THE MORE INTIMATE WE ARE WITH PEOPLE, THE MORE WE KNOW WHETHER WE CAN TRUST THEM OR NOT.

WE TRUST OR BELIEVE IN GOD IN DIRECT PROPORTION TO HOW MUCH WE HAVE GOT-TEN TO KNOW HIM. THE MORE INTIMATE WE ARE WITH HIM THE MORE WE KNOW THAT WE CAN TRUST HIM.

Our Source of Faith

To put it more concisely:

FAITH IN GOD PROCEEDS FROM INTIMACY WITH GOD! ***BUT HOW DO WE BECOME INTI-MATE WITH A GOD WE CAN'T SEE OR HEAR?***

That is a very important question and it has a very simple answer.

Every man, woman and child comes to this earth equipped with two complete sets of senses. One set is equipped to receive information from the physical or material world. The other set is equipped to receive information from the spiritual or non-material world. Whichever set of senses is exercised the most will dominate as our primary source of information.

When our spiritual senses are rejected as unreliable and ignored for long enough, they become like muscles that don't get used. They become weak and practically useless. The good news is that they don't go away. They are just waiting for some regular exercise to bring them back to life.

The spiritual senses pretty much parallel the natural senses.

1. Sight

We normally depend upon sight more than any other sense. We recognize people first by their appearance. We can identify our closest friends and family members from a distance by the way they walk or by other physical features.

The spiritual sense of sight can also be activated. Sometimes God visits people in a sovereign way, even when they are not actually seeking Him. Saul of Tarsus, (now known as the Apostle Paul) was blinded by a light coming from the person of Jesus. He was chosen for a specific call, and God knew that he was sincere in his zeal, even though he was not asking God for revelation. Paul later wrote in Hebrews 2:9, "But we see Jesus."

Of course, God also reveals Himself to those who earnestly seek Him. That is a consistent promise in the Bible, and I can certainly testify that it has worked for me and many others that I have known over the years. David wrote frequently in the Psalms how God heard his cry and answered him. In Psalm 46:1, he wrote that God was a "very present help in time of trouble." Jesus declared, "Seek and you shall find." Hebrews 12:1-2, states that we can run our race successfully if we keep "looking unto Jesus, the author and finisher of our faith."

In Acts 2, Peter quotes from Joel 3, declaring that in the

last days, many people would prophesy, see visions and dream dreams. Obviously, dreams and visions can be the spiritual sense of sight being utilized. I would suggest that everyone ask God to help them stir up this gift of spiritual sight, so they can see things from God's perspective. God has chosen to give some especially strong gifts of spiritual sight. These men and women and children are often called "seers."

2. Hearing

The sense of hearing is almost as important to us as the sense of sight, as most of our communication is received through this sense. Even so, most of our communication with God will be through our spiritual sense of hearing. Jesus said that the sheep know the voice of the shepherd. (John 10:4) Paul wrote that "Faith comes by hearing, and hearing by the word (rhema) of God." Romans 10:17.

The Voice and the Word

There is a difference between the voice and the words of a person. Sometimes it is just reassuring to hear the voice of the one we love, no matter what he or she is saying. But it's when we really listen to their words – what they are actually saying – that they can actually produce faith in us to believe what they say.

Recognizing the voice of the one who speaks is tremendously important for the building of our faith. If someone calls us on the phone and makes promises to us, but we don't recognize their voice and they don't tell us who they are, then we unlikely to believe them. But if we recognize the voice as someone we know and trust, then we can listen to their words and be confident that what they say is true.

The familiar voice gives us confidence to trust, and then the specific words give us the information we need for the application of that trust, as it becomes faith for a specific situation. We can trust someone, even if they don't tell us anything, but faith arises when they give us a verbal promise or commitment.

Thus, it's important, as God's sheep, to recognize Jesus' voice. There are so many other voices competing with His. Many are deceived, not recognizing the voice of their Beloved, because they haven't spent much time in His presence and don't know how to distinguish His voice from the others.

When we know His voice, then our spiritual ears perk up and we listen to what He has to say to us. That's where specific faith comes in for a particular application for our faith. It's really very simple. Spend time with Him, get to know His voice, and listen to what He has to say.

3. Sense of Touch

Touch is also a very wonderful sense. We feel comfort and love from those whose touch is precious to us. At other times we feel pain, which warns us to take action to avoid serious physical harm.

The spiritual sense of touch is also used in many ways, so we know who we can trust and who will bring us harm. Angelic beings are capable of touching us, even when we can't see them. Our hearts can be touched by both conviction and compassion. The Holy Spirit can touch us in powerful ways, even affecting our physical being. So many people in the world today have felt His power, especially when an anointed man or woman of God touches them.

We all enjoy being touched by someone who loves us. We can ask God to give us the ability to feel His Presence in a more powerful way. Supplementing our spiritual senses of sight and hearing is just one of the ways that God chooses to make Himself real to us.

4. Sense of Smell

While this is not as strong in humans as it is in dogs and many other animals, our lives are enriched by this special sense. The smell of bacon in the skillet or chocolate chip cookies in the oven can delight the one who enters the room. The smell of roses or carnations, favorite perfumes, etc., can bring nostalgic memories and create mental images of long-past joyful experiences.

Other smells can warn us of danger, such as the smell of smoke. This is a valuable function of the sense of smell. Without it, we could miss the fact that our house was on fire until it was too late to escape.

The spiritual sense of smell can be tied into the physical sense of smell for many people. My mother used to talk about a fragrance in the room when she worshipped. There was no explanation other than God was manifesting Himself in a way to delight her. God just loves to do things like that.

The spiritual sense of smell can also warn us of unseen and unclean beings in the atmosphere. There are people who smell demonic powers and fleshly attitudes and emotions, such as self-pity, anger and jealousy.

5. The Sense of Taste

"Oh taste and see that the Lord is good; Blessed is the man who trusts in Him!" (Psalm 34:8)

David is clearly calling on his readers to use their spiritual sense of taste to enjoy the greatness of God. Interestingly enough, the last part of the verse talks about faith or trust in God. The obvious implication is that if we use our spiritual senses to encounter God, our faith will be stronger, and we will be blessed as a result of it.

Again, let me try to make this as clear as possible:

1. We encounter God through spiritual senses, even as we encounter people through natural senses.
2. When we encounter God, our faith grows. We can see Him, hear Him, touch Him, smell Him and taste Him. It makes Him more and more real and we naturally trust Him more.
3. The result of our greater faith is great blessing in the form of miracles and answered prayer.

Our sense of taste gives us great pleasure throughout our lives. Our spiritual sense of taste is more abstract, but it relates to enjoying God's presence. Notice the word, pleasure, in the following passage:

"In Your presence is fullness of joy, at your right hand are pleasures for evermore." (Psalm 16:11b)

Earlier in this chapter, it was proposed that we all have two sets of senses – the natural senses and the spiritual senses. It was also suggested that they are like muscles that need to be used to stay productive. Clearly, most of us have depended much more upon our natural senses than our spiritual senses.

You may know a few people who are very much alive to the spiritual world. You might even think they are strange or weird if they see angels or demons and hear the voice of God. But perhaps, they have just been more in touch with their spiritual senses, while you may have been limited to your natural senses.

As my friend, Felito Utuie, from Mozambique teaches, Africans are very much aware of the spiritual realm, even if it is on the dark side. But in the western world, many are not in tune to either realm, and they have a hard time discerning what is going on in that realm.

I'd like to close this chapter with one of my favorite Scriptures.

> *"The Lord God has given me the tongue of the learned, that I should know how to speak a word in season to him who is weary. He awakens me morning by morning, **He awakens my ear to hear as the learned. The Lord God has opened my ear**, and I was not rebellious, nor did I turn away." (Isaiah 50:4, 5)*

In this passage, Isaiah is declaring that God has awakened and opened His ear. Obviously, He was not talking about natural ears, but spiritual ears.

If faith comes, at least in part, by hearing the "rhema" voice of God, then it would be a good thing to ask God to open and awaken our spiritual ears to hear that "rhema" word of God, not with our natural senses, but with our spiritual sense of hearing.

Just pray this simple prayer, repeating it as often as needed:

"Lord God, I want to hear your voice. Please awaken my spiritual ears this day and every day. May they remain open to hear your voice, that my faith in You might grow and increase for your Kingdom's sake. In Jesus' wonderful name, I pray. Amen!"

Chapter Six

Taking the Wrecking Ball to Our Structures of Unbelief

Just as any old building will not be totally demolished by one stroke of the wrecking ball, so our structures of unbelief may need repeated blows to completely destroy them. In this chapter, we will learn how to swing that wrecking ball for maximum results to bring down the different structures of unbelief that have been built into our lives over a long period of time.

Our Wrecking Ball

The wrecking ball God has given us is, of course, not physical, but spiritual. But it is not small or insignificant. It has all the backing of Heaven and it will do great damage to what the enemy has built in our hearts and lives.

This wrecking ball is not just the written Word of God, but

also God's words, which He has placed in our own mouths. Let's look at some of my favorite "wrecking ball" Scriptures.

In Isaiah 51, God is speaking to all His people, not just the prophet, Isaiah. That is clear from the first verse on. In verse 16 God declares:

> *"And I have put My words in your mouth; I have covered you with the shadow of My hand, that I may plant the heavens, lay the foundations of the earth, and say to Zion, 'You are My people.'" (Isaiah 51:16)*

This passage clearly implies that with the words God has put into our mouths, we can build and plant with Him. We clearly do this when we speak prophetic encouragement to others whom God connects us with.

But let's go to the next amazing Scripture in Jeremiah.

> *"Then the Lord put forth His hand and touched my mouth, and the Lord said to me: Behold, I have put My words in your mouth. See, I have this day set you over the nations and over the kingdoms, to root out and to pull down, to destroy and to throw down, to build and to plant." (Jeremiah 1:9, 10)*

As I look at this Scripture once again, I am visualizing the words that God has put in our mouths, coming out as wrecking balls, slamming into the stronghold structures of unbelief in our lives. As we get more specific with particular strongholds, it will help to build your faith if you remember this picture.

As the focus of Isaiah 51:16 was building and creating with

God, the first focus here in Jeremiah is the destruction of the old structures, before you build new ones. The other concept is rooting up negative and devilish plants and replacing them with positive, godly plants. The two are basically the same thing, but in this book, for the purpose of simplicity, we will focus on the building concept.

With that in mind, we can clearly see that when God puts His words in our mouths, we have the power to destroy any structures that the enemy has built. This is how it works:

1. For some reason, God has chosen to use us, who were created in His image and redeemed by the blood of His son, to speak His words on the earth, so that what He is declaring in Heaven will also be declared by us on the earth. When the words spoken on earth agree with those words spoken by God in Heaven, then the words have impact on the earth and Heaven rejoices with us.

2. These words can be creative or destructive. They can build a beautiful structure for God's presence, as when we praise and worship Him, or they can destroy the fortresses of the armies of hell. Of course, they must be God's words in God's timing, not our own words for our own selfish purposes.

3. Where the devil already has built structures of unbelief, we need to apply the wrecking ball of God's words to those structures, while we also begin to build structures of faith. The pattern in Jeremiah 1 is that we begin by tearing down the negative, thus making more room to build the positive.

As we begin to address the many types of structures of unbelief, we will get more specific in the wording that God has already given us to defeat these despicable structures the enemy has built into our lives and society. I am excited about the changes that will occur, as we apply these truths, and the miracles that will result because our faith has gone to new levels.

Before moving on, however, I want to answer a question that some readers will be asking. Where in the New Testament are we told that God puts His words in our mouths? That's a great question. Here is one verse that addresses it very powerfully:

> *"If anyone speaks, let him speak as the oracles of God. If anyone ministers, let him do it as with the ability which God supplies, that in all things God may be glorified through Jesus Christ, to whom belong the glory and the dominion forever and ever. Amen." (I Peter 4:11)*

Speaking as the oracles of God means you are speaking His words. In addition to this powerful command, we are also told by Paul to desire earnestly to prophesy and to desire spiritual gifts, but especially prophecy. (I Corinthians 14:1, 39) Almost the whole 14th chapter of I Corinthians deals with the power of prophecy to build and edify the body of Christ. It is one gift that is especially effective in building the faith of others and tearing down strongholds of unbelief.

Having both Peter and Paul making statements about speaking God's words is a powerful argument in favor of what we are talking about. But they just didn't talk about it, they practiced it. For instance, Peter and John, on their way to the temple at the hour of prayer, encountered the man who was lame from his mother's womb.

"And a certain man lame from his mother's womb was carried, whom they laid daily at the gate of the temple which is called Beautiful, to ask alms from those who entered the temple; who, seeing Peter and John about to go into the temple, asked for alms. And fixing his eyes on him, with John, Peter said, 'Look at us.' So he gave them his attention, expecting to receive something from them. Then Peter said, 'Silver and gold I do not have, but what I do have I give you; In the name of Jesus Christ of Nazareth, rise up and walk. And he took him by the right hand and lifted him up, and immediately his feet and ankle bones received strength. So he, leaping up, stood and walked and entered the temple with them walking, leaping, and praising God." (Acts 3:2-8)

Notice the process. Peter responded to an appeal for help by fixing his eyes on the man. While doing this, I am positive that he was listening to the Holy Spirit as to what to say to the lame man. First he said, "Look at us." That raised the man's expectation and faith. Then Peter shifted the man's focus from his short-term need to his greater need, and he spoke the words God was speaking to him. Then he declared that he was giving him the gift he really needed, which was a miracle from Heaven. Peter spoke the words that God put in his mouth, and as He spoke the words, Heaven and earth connected and the miracle happened.

Since faith comes by hearing the rhema of God, and since

Peter's words were the words of God, the lame man's faith was strengthened, and he responded as God brought the atmosphere of Heaven to earth. I'm sure you would agree that the lame man would not have been healed if Peter had not opened his mouth and spoken the words that God put in it.

Paul had a very similar experience while ministering in Lystra. In Acts 14:8-10, we read about another cripple from his mother's womb.

> *"And in Lystra a certain man without strength in his feet was sitting, a cripple from his mother's womb, who had never walked. This man heard Paul speaking. Paul, observing him intently and seeing that he had faith to be healed, said with a loud voice, 'Stand up straight on your feet!' And he leaped and walked."*

Notice that Paul also looked intently on the lame man, just as Peter had. It has been our experience in prophetic ministry, that often as you look on the face of the person who needs a word, that God will open up their soul to you as you look at them, especially as you look into their eyes – the windows of their soul.

The lame man had been listening to the words of Paul and faith was rising in his spirit. Surely, Paul was listening to the Holy Spirit as He spoke. As Paul focused on the lame man, God put His words in Paul's mouth, and the result again was a miracle.

Both Peter and Paul were also used to tear down and destroy the attempts of the enemy to hinder the progress of the Kingdom and the faith of its subjects.

Peter confronted Ananias and Sapphira in Acts 5 with

words of knowledge and God's judgment. I believe that God put His words in Peter's mouth when the conniving couple tried to deceive the servants of God. The result was the untimely death of the man and his wife. The greater result was that the awe of God increased, and the faith level grew, so that many more mighty signs and wonders were done. Read the whole chapter (Acts 5) for the details.

Paul did not speak a death sentence over anyone, but he did pronounce blindness to Elymas, the sorcerer, an enemy of the gospel, in Acts 13:8-12. Obviously, Heaven and earth came into agreement and Elymas was struck blind in response to the strong words of Paul against him.

Peter and Paul were indeed great examples in word and deed, but what about Jesus, Himself?

In John 12:48-50, Jesus clearly declared, as in other places, that He only spoke what the Father told Him to speak. In many places in the gospel of John, He also repeats that He is doing the works that His Father gave Him to do. He declared emphatically that He neither said nor did anything on His own, but He always did what His Father had instructed Him to do.

We also see in many stories of healing the lame, deaf and blind, etc. that He first spoke to the needy person, taking time to build their faith and overpower their structures of unbelief, before He provided the healing touch or declaration. One powerful example is the healing of the lame man at the pool in Jerusalem called Bethesda.

The man had a structure of unbelief and was filled with self-pity, saying that no one was there to help him get into the water when the angel stirred it. Jesus spoke faith into him and simply repeated the words His Father was speaking to Him and said, "Rise, take up your bed and walk." (John 5:8)

Before Jesus left His disciples, He talked to them about the coming of the Holy Spirit. One of the ministries of the Holy Spirit was teach them "all things" and remind them of "all things" that Jesus had spoken to them. (John 14:26) Since Jesus only spoke what His Father had spoken first, we know that the Holy Spirit, Who has come to live within us (John 14:17), is here to let us know what the Father and Son are both saying now in Heaven.

Let me reiterate that when we agree on earth with what is being spoken in Heaven, we can declare and decree the same way that Peter and Paul did, and Heaven will back our words with powerful results.

Let's also remember that our focus is the removal of the structures of unbelief, using God's powerful wrecking ball – the words that He puts in our mouths. The starting point and guiding light is the written word that we've been given and call the Holy Bible. It is the standard by which we can discern that which is of God and that which is not. But we are also given the Holy Spirit, Who lives within us, and He can speak to our hearts and minds specific words, declarations and decrees for any particular situation we or others are facing.

Now let's begin the campaign to tear down and destroy those nasty structures of unbelief that have been erected in our lives.

Chapter Seven

Crushing the Tower of Fear

As discussed in an earlier chapter, fear is a monster, and in the majority of people worldwide, it dictates an enormous amount of words and actions. Along with fear's assistants – anxiety, worry and insecurity – this terrible despot creates many mental and physical health problems for its subjects.

But God's Word always provides the answers that we need. Indeed, even against this enemy, which is like a tower of evil strength in our lives, "We are more than conquerors." (Romans 8:37)

One common fear that Christians have is the fear of exercising spiritual gifts. Paul addressed that fear when he wrote Timothy in II Timothy 1:6-7. He then gave Timothy a three-barreled shotgun to put his fear to flight, or, to use our previous analogy, he provided three big wrecking balls to crush this ungodly tower of devilish strength. This is the passage:

*"Therefore I remind you to stir up the gift of God which
is in you through the laying on of my hands. For God has
not given us the spirit of fear, but of power and of love and
of a sound mind."*

First of all, we need to face our fear head on. We need
to discern when anxiety, worry or feelings of insecurity begin
to slip into our thinking. We would be wise to ask a spouse
or close friend to help us recognize these insidious enemies.
Sometimes they sneak up on us, but others can see them coming before we do.

When we become aware that we are being attacked, we
need to raise our shield of faith, knowing that "if God is for us,
who can be against us?" (Romans 8:31) With authority, we can
rebuke the spirit of fear that is attacking us by binding it and
breaking its power over us.

When we have done this, we are ready to take the wrecking
balls, given to us by Paul, to crush the structure of fear that our
enemy has been building and hiding in.

1. Power

God did not give us a spirit of fear, but He did give us the
Spirit of Power – the Holy Spirit. This dunamis power is a great
antidote for fear, because fear is the feeling that you have no
power. But Jesus said, "You will receive power, when the Holy
Spirit has come upon you." (Acts 1:8) Power from the Holy
Spirit overpowers fear and crushes it.

Thus, after we recognized the fear and rebuked it, we need
to claim and proclaim that we have received the "Spirit of Power",

and let the devil know that he is no match for the power of God's Holy Spirit dwelling in us.

2. Love

John, the Beloved, was known for how much he loved the Lord Jesus Christ. His gospel and his epistles are filled with references to love. But one of the most famous verses from I John reveals another wrecking ball to crush the tower of fear in our lives.

"There is no fear in love; but perfect love casts out fear." (I John 4:18)

How does that work? First of all, this perfect love, which is God's "agape" love, is supernatural – the fruit of the Holy Spirit. It comes upon us just like the "power" comes upon us. It causes us to focus totally on the person in need, rather than on ourselves.

Fear is usually self-centered. It's about our potential pain or loss. Love is others centered. When the love of the Holy Spirit causes us to focus on the other person, the fear departs from our minds and hearts.

Secondly, when we receive God's love and feel His arms surrounding us, it takes away the insecurity that is a part of our fear. So whether the fear relates to our own needs, or the need to minister to others, we can defeat this enemy by declaring that we have received this wonderful fruit of God's Holy Spirit, and fear must go in the name of Jesus.

3. A Sound Mind

Fear causes a troubled or unhealthy mind. It brings confusion and physical illness. A sound mind is a healthy mind – a mind that thinks clearly and logically to a reasonable conclusion. This also is a gift from God.

Many troubled minds have resulted from past pain and loss. The damaged emotions need to be healed and restored to be able to maintain the sound mind that God has given to us. I believe it would be wise for us to seek some Godly inner-healing, such as "sozo", Elijah House, or prophetic deliverance. Jesus, the Good Shepherd, "restores my soul", but He often uses other members of His body to bring healing to His body.

The Greek word for "sound mind" comes from a word meaning to "return to one's senses" or "disciplined mind".

I believe that this is also a gift of God that we can ask for and receive by faith. Those whose minds are troubled with anxiety, worry and fear can boldly proclaim and decree that God has already given us a sound mind, and we will not tolerate the attacks from the enemy. Instead, we declare that we are hurling this wrecking ball from Heaven and destroying this hellish structure in our lives.

Additional Strategies to Destroy the Tower of Fear

1. Meditate on the Psalms

David and other writers of the Psalms were very open and honest with their feelings and troubles, and it is easy to identify with their worries and fears. But they always sandwiched their troubles with bold statements that God was their strong tower, and He already had given them victory or surely would give them victory. They expressed their fears honestly, but attacked them boldly with the word of God and their own testimonies of past deliverances from their enemies.

If fear is an issue you deal with on a regular basis, you should spend time with David in the Psalms as frequently as possible. Begin to memorize some of the verses that speak to you the most powerfully. There are scores of such psalms and they are not hard to find. Almost every psalm has verses that will build your faith and help you destroy the structure of fear in your life.

2. Accountability

Every time we humble ourselves to ask for help and accountability, we receive another portion of God's grace. (James 4:6). All God's blessings come through His grace. Asking a spouse or friend to hold us accountable is a great strategy to conquer this enemy and destroy this demonic structure of fear.

3. Recognize Fear as Sin and Repent

While fear is a satanic attack on our soul, when we accept and agree with it we should accept that as sin and repent of it. "Whatever is not from faith is sin." (Romans 14:23). Fear is actually an insult to God. It says, "I don't think you love me enough nor have enough power to help me in my situation." Fear and faith are direct opposites, and they are incompatible in the same place at the same time.

If you have allowed fear to take root and build structures in your life, simply ask God to forgive you for agreeing with the enemy. Then accept His forgiveness and don't remind Him again.

Asking for Grace and Favor

Then, immediately after humbling yourself and asking forgiveness, ask Him for more grace. Claim that promise of James 4:6. Grace will enable you to trust Him more. Then ask Him for favor; favor also comes with grace. Then after asking for favor, make a declaration and decree as a king or queen, serving the King of kings.

Repentance and humility actually are wonderful keys to blessing and prosperity. Whenever we have the opportunity to humble ourselves, before God or anyone in our lives, we should take advantage of that opportunity. I know it's hard to do at first, but with practice, it gets much easier and the rewards are amazing! When we find ourselves in that humble place where we have just asked for mercy, which we know we didn't deserve, we are in the perfect place to ask for more favor, which we also don't feel like we deserve.

But God sees the tenderness in our hearts, and He desires to show His love and appreciation as we humble ourselves before Him and others. It's a time for Him to pull some strings and open doors for us, or pull out His checkbook and write us a nice bonus for serving Him faithfully. This sounds like the opposite of humility – asking for favor and blessings when you just confessed that you did something wrong – but it's really an extension of humility, because you are humbling yourself and admitting that you need favor, rather than being so independent that you won't ask for help.

Of course, we don't repent for selfish reasons, but when we

truly humble ourselves, we should follow the biblical pattern I saw in the book of Ruth. Our book, *The Boaz Blessing*, explains this in greater detail. God is actually very pleased when we do ask for favor, because it gives Him a chance to show us that He is a good and giving God, and it gives us a good reason to put our trust in Him. If He blesses us immediately after we did something offensive to Him and confessed it, we know how great a God He really is.

Sample Prayer of Repentance

"Dear Father, I come in Jesus' name to confess that I've allowed Your enemy to build a structure of fear in my heart and soul. I also confess that my natural ancestors have also allowed the same structures of fear in their own lives and passed them on to me. I repent for accepting Your enemy's lies and not believing Your promises of love and protection. I am sorry for offending You by not fully accepting and receiving these wonderful gifts from Your gracious hand.

Thank you, Father, for accepting my confession and for totally forgiving me for allowing fear to dominate my life and overrule Your promises to me. I ask for Your continued help to recognize the lies of Satan and his attempts to bring fear back into my life. I pray these things in the wonderful name of Your beloved Son, Jesus Christ. Amen!"

Sample Petition for Favor

"And now, Father, would You show me favor as I walk into this new freedom from fear? Would You show me a

*special token of Your love by supplying a need in my life
and also help me to help someone else with the same needs
that I have experienced? I will give You glory, honor and
praise."*

Sample Declaration and Decree

*"I am making a declaration and a decree that I renounce
and reject all fear, anxiety, worry and insecurity. I declare
that I am beloved of my Father, and He cares deeply for
my safety, security and provision. I proclaim that I am
chosen by Him to impact others by using the faith He has
given me to bring transformation into their lives, including their natural and spiritual health and prosperity."*

4. Read Biographies of Men and Women of Faith

There is something about reading the stories of men and
women of faith that can touch your spirit in such a way that
you will never be the same. The testimonies of others can overpower your fear with an "If they can do it, so can I" attitude.

There are so many books available. Some of the greatest
post-biblical stories include George Mueller, Rees Howells,
David Livingston, Gladys Aylward, David Yongi Cho, Heidi
Baker and so many more. An internet search for "biographies
men and women of faith" will bring up well over a million
responses. The resources are so abundant that there is enough
material provided to read a different biography every week or
so for the rest of your life!

Chapter Eight

Destroying Structures of False Science and Bad Doctrine

I t is now time to take our wrecking balls to false science and bad doctrine. True science is a blessing to the human race and the whole earth. But false science and proud intellectualism, along with false doctrine, have been incredibly destructive, causing great loss to the Kingdom of Heaven. They have hindered the free flow of signs and wonders on the earth, by building strong structures of unbelief in the lives of Christian "believers." In addition, potential believers have had mental hurdles to overcome because of the structures of false science built in their souls by unbelieving teachers and professors.

False Science

In order to dismantle and destroy the structures of unbelief created by false science, we need to define what true science is and what false science is. Science is an enormous topic with many different sub-topics, such as biology, physics, chemistry, natural science, geology, zoology and many more. Then you can break each one down into sub-sub-topics, such as nuclear physics, quantum physics, biochemistry, electrochemistry, etc. But in spite of the quantity and variety of the different subjects classified as science, we can still come up with a simple definition of what science is.

The basic definition of science, as I would define it, is: ***the observation, gathering and organization of information about any material substance, living and non-living in the universe.***

Wikipedia defines it this way: ***"Science (from Latin scientia, meaning "knowledge") is a systematic enterprise that builds and organizes knowledge in the form of testable explanations and predictions about the universe."***

What About Evolution?

The theory of evolution qualifies as para-science because it is a theory, and is therefore not pure science. The word, "testable" in the above Wikipedia definition disqualifies it from being true science. There is no way to test this theory, and there is no one who has observed evolution taking place. We do find and study fossils, bones and artifacts, but we can only extrapolate so much from them.

We know that species can adapt to their environment to a certain degree, but we have never observed a species being transformed into another species. The fact is that the more we discover about genetics and DNA, the more problems it creates for honest scientists who want to explain and believe in evolution. The fact is: species remain in their family and do not migrate to another family of species.

It is not the object of this book to fully refute the theory of evolution. There are many wonderful books by outstanding scientists who list the contradictions to the theory of evolution in the scientific data. For more information, enter "Creationism" or "Creation Science" in any internet search engine.

An Interesting Debate

I had some fun a few years ago, after attending a Creationism Seminar, which listed numerous arguments against the theory of evolution. I began to write letters to the editor in our small town newspaper, the Willapa Harbor Herald. They didn't have too much going on there, so they printed my letter. A university professor from another city read my letter and was not thrilled with my statements. He wrote a response to the editor in which he tried to intimidate me with his credentials and scientific arguments. I responded with more facts from the seminar notebook.

We went back and forth for several weeks. I may not have convinced the professor to give up the theory of evolution, but something else happened that let me know that the theory of evolution's foundation is very shaky. We had a high school teacher in the church where Brenda and I pastored, and he informed me of a conversation he had with one of the science teachers in the school.

This man, like many in the community, had read our back and forth communications. What I had written in my letters had shaken him to the core, to the point that he wasn't sleeping at night. He kept thinking about the anti-evolution arguments that he had never heard. Obviously, they actually made sense to him, but left him in a dilemma, not knowing what to believe.

If it Wasn't *So* Devastating it Would be Humorous!

While I was having fun at the time, I realized that, like many theological debates, we were not just talking about who's right and who's wrong. We were talking about a false science doctrine that has been instrumental in the escalation of doubt, unbelief and the degradation of our western society.

Evolution is false science and is overwhelmingly taught not as a theory, but as a fact. Check out any textbook or science program on TV, and they will treat evolution as a proven historical fact, like the Alamo or the Vietnam War. The unspoken, but devastating implication is: We don't need religion anymore, because we don't need God to explain our existence or the existence of our planet.

Instead, if we subscribe to the Darwinian theory, we have the wonderful, incredible fact that when nothing at all existed, suddenly nothing exploded into something and became a huge universe filled with galaxies, stars and planets. Then non-living matter spontaneously breathed on itself the breath of life and became a living cell. Then, through a series of accidents, that actually made something better, living cells learned how to multiply and develop complex parts. Somewhere during the course of billions of years, an eye was accidently formed with its incredibly complex parts. The brain and nervous system miraculously formed with all the complexity of a multitude of computers.

Of course, the whole theory is preposterous, but sinful human beings love and embrace it, not because there is evidence for it, but simply because it means they don't have to believe in the Creator anymore. This gives them freedom to do whatever feels good at the time. As long as they can get away with it on the earth, there won't be a day of reckoning when this life is over. This theory has been a very close business partner with religious humanism, and together they have taken the mountain of education by storm.

Confronting the Lie

The more formal education we receive, the bigger the unbelief structures will be. As Paul declared, "Knowledge puffs up." (I Corinthians 8:1). We unconsciously breathe in the intellectual pride that pervades academic institutions. I only have a master's degree, with six years of college and university life, but that was enough to experience the ego exaltation in the environment of each campus. Even Bible colleges or seminaries have their share of intellectual or theological pride.

This pride is the open door for the enemy to come in and build his structures of doubt and unbelief. Since "God resists the proud," it's logical that the enemy actually embraces the proud and finds the doorway into their soul wide open.

The first lie we should confront is the lie that we are so well-informed that we don't really need the Bible that much. The lie says that it may have a lot of good teaching, but scientifically, it really is outdated and not relevant to our academic world.

Without God's Word as our foundation, we build on quicksand. We must hold His Word in high regard. It was not written as a science textbook, but it contains scientific secrets and nuggets of revelation. Some of it may need interpretation and clarification for our understanding, but what is written is true and protected from error by the Holy Spirit.

Step One: Prayer of Repentance

I would therefore, highly encourage anyone with a higher education to ask God's forgiveness for having pride in their education and intelligence and for feeling superior to those who lack that level of education. We can confess our desire to appear wise and intelligent to others and to be right, while proving the other person wrong. We can confess that we haven't placed enough value on the Word of God. We may have read many pages of man's wisdom, while neglecting the Wisdom from Above, as recorded in the Bible.

It's not just evolution we are dealing with here. You may have never bought into the theory at all. But you may have allowed intellectual pride to puff you up to where you felt less dependent on God and His people. You may have a good income, because of your education and training, which is a good thing in and of itself, but it can easily lead to pride that God must resist. The best idea is to humble yourself before God and He promises to exalt you. Thus, I encourage you again; take every opportunity to humble yourself and confess any possible weaknesses. The promises of God to the humble are too awesome to leave them all for someone else. I'd sure like to get my share of them, so I'm ready to confess and repent whenever I have a chance.

Point of Clarification

Please understand, I'm not saying we shouldn't develop our intellect and expand our knowledge. While writing this portion, I have interrupted myself long enough to play a game of internet scrabble with my brilliant son, Nathan. We like to compete and challenge each other. I also love to admire his creativity and strategy. We stimulate each other's brain functions, which is a great thing. But God does help us to keep humble hearts and honor each other as we play. We don't feel threatened or intimidated by each other's intelligence. And, of course, I think that's the way it should be.

Step Two: Arm Yourself

Your most powerful weapon is the Word of God. For example, Psalm 119 is the longest chapter in the Bible with 176 verses, but almost every single verse has a reference to the written words of God that were available to King David at the time of his writings. He exalts the words of God over the words of all his other teachers.

Another wonderful passage is Proverbs 2, talking about wisdom, knowledge and understanding. Verse 6 says: *"For the Lord gives wisdom; From His mouth comes knowledge and understanding."* Much of the book talks about God's superior wisdom.

One great New Testament passage is I Corinthians 2, which reveals that the wisdom of God is far superior to the wisdom of men. Paul talks about the mysteries of God, which are only revealed to those who walk in the Spirit. To the natural man, the wisdom of God makes no sense, but to the spiritual man, it is far superior to natural wisdom.

Romans 1 also provides some insight for us as to how supposedly wise men became so foolish. Romans 1:22 says, *"Professing to be wise, they became fools."* I can certainly see how that fits the evolutionists.

In addition to reading the Bible, I would encourage everyone again to look up some of the amazing literature on Creationism. It will really open your eyes to how the Word of God is actually being confirmed by scientific data. For instance, only the biblical account of Noah's flood can explain many phenomena of geology, etc.

Chapter Nine

Crushing the False Gods
in Our Lives

In Chapter Four, we listed eight different common idols in our western world. These idols affect Christians as well as unbelievers. The eight we looked at were:

1. Government
2. Medical Science
3. Insurance
4. Money, Investments, etc.
5. Education
6. Friends, Family and Allies
7. Unions
8. Entertainment

We won't take the time to address each of these in great

detail, one-on-one, as the same principles apply to each one that has affected our lives. What we will do is focus on the heart issues that need to be understood and dealt with.

The Number One Issue

We serve a loving Father and He totally understands our culture and the challenges we face. He knows how difficult it is to always "get it right", when it comes to dealing with our challenges. He is not comparing our journey to someone in Africa or India who lives in poverty and never has to deal with the pride of education, or trust in doctors, education or insurance. God lives with us in our culture, just like He lives with them in theirs. So let me say this boldly: **GOD UNDERSTANDS YOU!**

Therefore, He wants to speak peace to your heart, rather than condemnation, shame and guilt. It is true that faith does not come easily, because of so many false idols available to us, but it is also true that He can give us the grace to rise above the challenges we face. Yes, He can and will give His children the faith they ask for, if they will come to Him with humble hearts, and ask Him to help them.

As we applied the wrecking ball to the structures of fear and false teachings, both secular and sacred, so we will apply the same wrecking ball to the false gods we have served in the past. This of course, does not mean completely dropping out of our western culture, but it does mean changing the way we think and act concerning our western culture.

Refreshing the Soul Through Repentance

Before we get into some practical wisdom regarding how we handle these western cultural issues, let's deal with the first obvious and necessary steps to demolishing this structure of unbelief. We must first come with humble hearts to acknowledge and confess the fact that we have put some of our faith and confidence in false gods that should have been placed in the One True God.

We might pray something like this:

"Dear Father in Heaven,

It has been pointed out to me that I have been raised in a culture that has placed a lot of faith and trust in natural and human idols. I am a part of that culture and I am also guilty of that sin against You. I humbly ask for Your forgiveness and Your mercy, and I repent and turn from that way of living. I ask for Your wisdom and Your help to change the way I think and act in the future. I so want to please You, and I realize that without faith it is impossible to please You. I really want my faith to be totally in You, Father, and I know that I can't have the faith I desire, while I put so much trust in other western idols.

Thank you for forgiving me and helping me! I give you all the glory for all that You will accomplish through me. In Jesus' name, Amen!"

When you pray that prayer or something like it in your own words, God totally cleanses and forgives you, and you can start over with a clean slate.

Making the Necessary Adjustments:
Thoughts and Attitudes

The way we think determines the way we act and guides our destiny. We must get our thought life under the control of the Holy Spirit. We must be led by the Holy Spirit in every area of our life to truly walk with God. It's not enough to be led by the Spirit when we minister to someone. We need to be led by the Holy Spirit when we make little decisions, which often are much more consequential than we ever expected them to be.

What should I think about government, insurance, doctors, unions, investments, etc.? We know they are not evil in themselves; any more than a piece of wood or a rock or the sun, etc., is evil in itself. It's when they become an object we look to for something that God has already promised to provide for us that they take on a cloak of evil.

I believe that the very best person to ask such questions of is God, Himself. We really want to know what He thinks and what we should think about these potential idols in our lives. We can come to Him with faith that He will answer, because it's the question He has been waiting for us to ask. It is in our intimate walk with Him that we can just say, "God, what do you think about me going to the doctor for this issue or this concern? What do you think about me accepting this handout from the government? Should I have more or less insurance?"

When you clearly hear God's voice (usually a still, small one in your spirit), you are much more likely to give God the glory and not the potential idol in your world. The secret, which I believe is a bit of fresh revelation from God, is to make God a part of every decision by asking Him and listening for His answer. We don't need any more rules, such as: "Don't get insurance! Don't pay your taxes! Don't accept food stamps! Don't invest for your future!" God doesn't want us to walk by rules and commandments under the New Covenant. We want to write them on our hearts – He wants to speak to our heart when we have a question.

When we involve Him from start to finish with the doctor, the financial planner, the government assistance program, the insurance agent, etc., it pleases God greatly, and assures Him that we are putting our faith in Him and His advice, rather than the human beings that He might use to bless us. Yes, He will often say "Yes" to our using the resources that our society has made available to us.

However, we must also be aware and ready to agree with Him when He asks us to step out of the boat and walk on water, instead of doing the natural and logical thing. We may look foolish to others, but if God has spoken, we can have total confidence that He will come through for us. However, if we take steps out of our own pride and self-confidence, without really hearing from God, we may be actually doing something foolish. This is where intimacy comes in; we know the voice of our best friend and life partner.

My own favorite way to hear God's voice is to open my Bible and start reading. I may turn many pages before something really speaks to me. On the other hand, I often get an answer on the very first page and the very first verse I look at.

Others may just rest quietly before the Lord, listening to intimate worship music until they feel the sweet presence of Almighty God, coming with His ministering angels, and the comfort of the Holy Spirit. They hear Him whisper their name and He tells them what's on His mind.

There is nothing that will build your faith in God more than hearing His voice, as we discussed earlier. Hearing God's voice becomes easier, as you become more intimate with Him. In other words, the more intimate we become, the more our faith will grow. We've stated that before, but it bears much repetition, because it is so important. Shortcuts to faith usually produce very little. Faith that flows out of intimacy with God produces an abundant life full of fruit and miracles.

As we deal a crushing blow to the structures of unbelief and build our intimate relationship with the Father, Son and Holy Spirit, we will see miracles increase more and more. It's not a quick fix, but it is a sure path to a truly exciting and fulfilling life in the Kingdom.

Some Practical Guidelines

The following are not rules to follow. They are some guidelines to think about in making various decisions. Ultimately, you want to hear from God and feel His peace before making any decision.

1. Regarding government.

The longstanding trend in America, and most western nations, has been for the government to grow bigger and bigger, while individual freedoms decrease from year-to-year and administration-to-administration. We know this is very detrimental to a life of adventure with God, and the freedom we need to help us spread His gospel around the world. Thus, I would lean towards decisions that would decrease the need for government, rather than increase it, but every situation is different. Some will have faith for greater independence, but some are not there yet.

2. Regarding Doctors, Medicine, Insurance, Unions etc.

My recommendation would be to ask the Lord how much we can do without, when it comes to these forms of security. In any case, what we do use of their benefits, we should always give the glory to God for leading us to the right person or policy. *We give thanks to others, but give the glory to God.*

The right attitude should be something like this: *"I asked God for His wisdom to help me in this situation. God answered and led me to the right person or policy that was just what I needed for this situation. God is so Awesome! He cares about every detail of my life!"*

This declaration of our testimony takes the focus off the natural provision and puts it on our Supernatural Provider, removing the idolatry from our hearts and minds. This does not mean we shouldn't be very grateful to others that God uses to help us. We can thank them graciously, but give the greater glory to God who created them and gave them their talents.

3. Regarding Education

This is a highly individual decision. There are some people through whom God wants to show off, like He did through his apostles. In Acts 4:13, we read how the leaders were amazed at the apostles' boldness, knowing they were uneducated men, but they realized that they had been with Jesus.

Some of you may be powerful examples of this yourself. You may not have much formal education, but your spiritual gifts more than make up for that. I'm reminded of a pastor's wife in Mozambique, Africa. Heidi Baker related to us that although she couldn't pass her exams at the Bible School they offered, it was hard to give her a failing grade when she had already raised several people from the dead.

Others of you may have dreams of getting a great education, so you can go to the top of whatever mountain God places you on. For you, especially, I recommend my two books: *Kings and Kingdoms* and *Finding Your Place on Your Kingdom Mountain*.

I didn't have much ambition for a higher education, as I wanted to get into "the ministry" as soon as possible. But God spoke to me to take the seminary program, which involved going to a secular university for my first degree. Following that, I kept going until I had the Master's degree that would open more doors for me and mature my mind for a teaching ministry that I didn't know I had at the time.

The important thing for me then, and now, was and is the ability to hear God's voice. In those days, I was having a great personal awakening, and I knew God had spoken to me. Not long after that, I heard God's voice again as I sought Him about the decision of marriage. Once again, He made it perfectly clear that He had put Brenda in my life; she would be a great blessing to me, and I could help her achieve her own destiny.

4. Regarding People We Trust

It's wonderful to have supporting people around us, and we are especially thankful for the Body of Christ – the church.

Clearly, our attitude once again must be that God has given them to us to help us. They receive our thanks, but God gets all the glory for making it happen.

However, please also be cautioned; not everyone that comes into our lives, or even our churches, is necessarily sent from God. Paul made that very clear in Acts 20:29: *"For I know this, that after my departure, savage wolves will come in among you, not sparing the flock."*

That is why each of us needs to be continually communing with the Lord, and as advised in Proverbs 3:6, *"In all your ways acknowledge Him and He shall direct your paths."*

We need to know God and His voice if we want to be protected. We also need others who we can trust to help us discern the difference between the sheep and the wolves that come in sheep's clothing. God has put all the necessary gifts in the church, but many have lain dormant and unused; they need to be stirred up and not neglected, as Paul exhorted Timothy in I Timothy 4:14 and II Timothy 1:6-7.

5. Regarding Entertainment

I believe God wants us to enjoy many healthy forms of entertainment and not be so spiritually minded that we can't relate to anyone on earth. At the same time, it has been so easy to get our comfort and mental relief from this aspect of western life, instead of getting our comfort and mental relief from God, Himself. In many ways it's like "comfort food", which could have been included as one of the real idols in our western society and culture. We usually like the two of them together, and surely most of us indulge too much in both food and entertainment.

Again, the answer is talking and listening to God about these possible idols in our lives. We need to get His opinion of our own situations.

Some people are called to the entertainment mountain. Thus, entertainment, such as acting, singing, dancing or sports may be very important to them. They learn things while they watch, so they can accomplish more themselves. We must be slow to judge others, because we don't know everything that God has planned for them, no matter how prophetic we may be.

God does know what He has planned for you, and yes, He can speak to you. Claim the statement made by Isaiah in Isaiah 50:4, a verse that was quoted earlier in the book:

> *"The Lord God has given me the tongue of the learned, that I should know how to give a word in season to him who is weary. He wakens me morning by morning; He awakens my ear to hear as the learned."*

This verse is obviously talking about hearing God's voice to encourage others, but clearly, He can also open our ears to give us wisdom for decisions that we need to make on our journey.

Declaration and Decree

Here is a sample declaration and decree that you can make to nullify the effect of false idols that have robbed you of your faith in God in times past.

> *"Today, in Jesus' name, I declare and decree that I will not look to any false idol for my source of security, provision*

or comfort. Everything I receive comes either directly or indirectly from my loving Father in Heaven. He cares for my every need and directs my paths, so that I can stay in the center of His will for my life and destiny. I refuse to see the government, insurance, doctors, medicine, money, education, friends and family, unions or entertainment as the source of anything I need. If God blesses me with any of these, then I give Him all the glory for providing for me. Whether they are in my life or not, He will take care of me, because He is my One and Only True Provider and the Source of everything of value in my life. Amen!

Chapter Ten

Some Final Thoughts

My thoughts and meditations were briefly interrupted by our precious granddaughter, Tyrza, who wanted me to play catch with the balloons Brenda had gotten for her. They had just returned from their long stroller walk on this beautiful September morning by the lake in Peachland, BC, Canada. My mind drifts back in time to that early morning hour when Tyrza's mom, our then sixteen-year-old daughter, Andrea, woke up in the night with a severe asthma attack.

It was about 4 AM when we took Andrea to our small-town hospital, where she was given a treatment and sent home, without seeing a doctor. After the twelve-mile ride home, she began to struggle to breathe again and we rushed her back to the hospital. This time, she had completely stopped breathing on her own. While I drove as fast as I could, navigating the bay-shore winding road on the coast of Washington State, Brenda breathed her own breath hard into Andrea's lungs, not realizing that her lungs had actually collapsed at that time. Her body stiffened up and we learned later that she had suffered a cardiac arrest.

While we drove, we both cried out to God and reminded Him of the words she had received concerning her destiny and her role in a harvest of souls for the Kingdom. We took the wrecking ball of God's words and promises to demolish the fear we felt attacking our souls. We were doing warfare with the prophetic words God had given us (I Timothy 1:18).

When we arrived at the hospital, they rushed Andrea into the emergency room and prepared to take drastic action. Before they asked us both to leave the room, we saw Andrea's hand move, indicating that life had come back to her and that God had heard our prayers. The medical team had not actually done anything yet.

Thankfully, Andrea recovered without drastic surgery, etc. She graduated from our Christian School and went on to college, graduating from Christ For The Nations Institute in Dallas, Texas. While there, she fulfilled many of the words that had been spoken over her, including the development of her gifts in the field of drama and evangelism.

When an accident or other emergency happens to you or your family, how prepared is your faith to believe for the miracle that you desperately need? If we hadn't been taught how to grow our faith, through the Word of God and the words given to us personally by His servants, we don't know what would have happened to our daughter.

We never know when someone else will have an emergency. It could be someone we know and love, or it could be someone we've never met. We might be the first person at an accident scene, where lives hang in the balance, and it's up to us and the faith that God has given us. At that time, it's a little late to work on building faith, but we can still ask the Holy Spirit to breathe His life through us and touch the body of the accident victim.

In the meantime, why not prepare ourselves for events that happen to us on the journey of life? Why not wage a good warfare against the faith destroyers in our lives? Let's make the effort to swing that wrecking ball of God's Word at the structures of fear and unbelief that our enemy has been building in our souls.

I encourage you to copy some of the prayers, declarations and decrees from this book that apply to your situation. Print them up and place them where you can read them on a daily basis. Faith is a precious possession, worth more to you than gold or silver, stocks or bonds. It will get you out of trouble better than a high-priced attorney, and faith will give you peace of mind better than any insurance policies or sleeping pills.

It's only those with His faith that can please Him. He gives His faith to those who ask for it and pursue a relationship with Him.

With faith you can move the mountains in your world. Without faith, you can't move anything significant.

How long has the enemy robbed you of your faith through fear, lies and false securities? How much longer are you going to put up with it?

I encourage each reader to make God a promise something like this:

Dear Father God,

By Your grace, I am going to demolish every stronghold of unbelief in my life, using the Words that You have spoken to me. I will rebuke every fear and lie from Satan and

I will take down every idol and false security god in my life. I will not give Your glory to government, insurance, medical science, investments, education, special people in my life, unions or entertainers. I will give You all the glory and honor for life, health, provision, relationships, success and general happiness. I am Yours and forever shall be! I long to hear Your voice more clearly and experience Your love more fully. I desire to use the faith that You have given me to do exploits for You and to build Your Kingdom. For this reason, Lord, I ask for your wisdom and strength to take down all structures of unbelief and grant me the opportunity to grow and strengthen the faith that pleases You and brings glory to Your name.

In Jesus' precious name!

Amen!

I sincerely hope and pray that this small book will have a big impact on your life. Your faith is one of the most powerful weapons you could ever possess. I pray that as a result of what you have learned here, your name will be added to the Heavenly expanded version of Hebrews 11 – The Hall of Faith.

Ben Peters

BEN R. PETERS has been a student of the Word since he could read it for himself. He has a heritage of grandparents and parents who lived by faith and taught him the value of faith. That faith produced many miracle answers to prayer in their family life. Ben and Brenda have founded a ministry in northern Illinois called Kingdom Sending Center. They also travel extensively world-wide, teaching and ministering prophetically to thousands annually. Their books are available on most e-readers, as well as their website: *www.kingdomsendingcenter.org* and all other normal book outlets.

The Ultimate Convergence
An End Times Prophecy of the Greatest
Shock and Awe Display Ever to Hit Planet Earth
by Ben R. Peters

Available from Kingdom Sending Center
www.kingdomsendingcenter.org

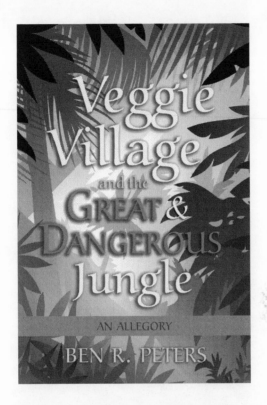

**Veggie Village and the Great
and Dangerous Jungle**
An Allegory
by Ben R. Peters

Available from Kingdom Sending Center
www.kingdomsendingcenter.org

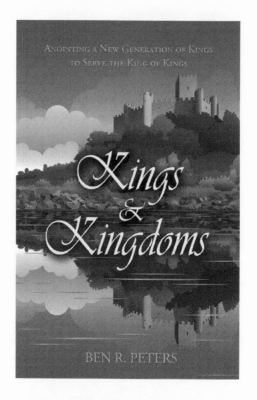

Kings and Kingdoms
Anointing a New Generation of Kings
to Serve the King of Kings
by Ben R. Peters

Available from Kingdom Sending Center
www.kingdomsendingcenter.org

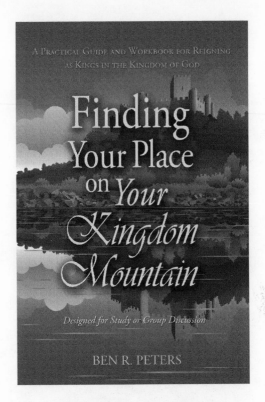

Finding Your Place
on Your Kingdom Mountain
A Practical Guide and Workbook for Reigning
as Kings in the Kingdom of God
by Ben R. Peters

Designed for Study or Group Discussion

Available from Kingdom Sending Center
www.kingdomsendingcenter.org

Catching up to the Third World
Seven Indispensable Keys
To EXPLOSIVE Revival
in the Western Church
by Ben R. Peters

Available from Kingdom Sending Center
www.kingdomsendingcenter.org

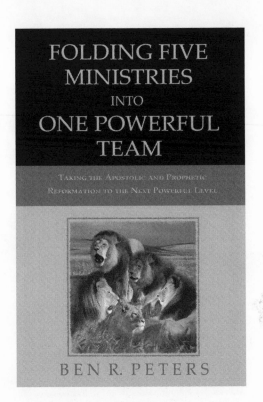

Folding Five Ministries Into
One Powerful Team
Taking the Apostolic and Prophetic Reformation
to the Next Powerful Level
by Ben R. Peters

Available from Kingdom Sending Center
www.kingdomsendingcenter.org

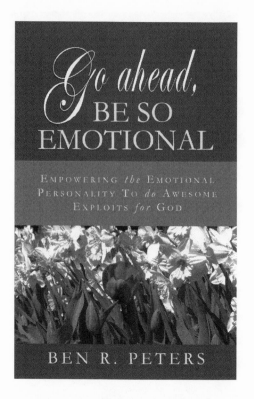

Go Ahead, Be So Emotional
Empowering the Emotional Personality
to do Awesome Exploits for God
by Ben R. Peters

Available from Kingdom Sending Center
www.kingdomsendingcenter.org

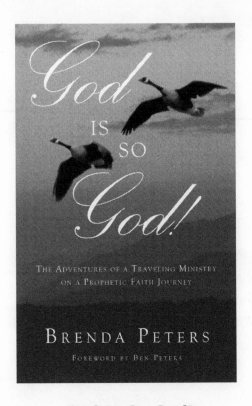

God Is So God!
The Adventures of a Traveling Ministry
on a Prophetic Faith Journey
by Brenda Peters

Available from Kingdom Sending Center
www.kingdomsendingcenter.org

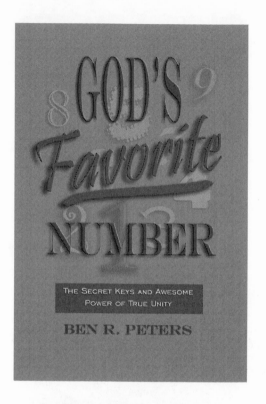

God's Favorite Number
The Secret Keys and Awesome
Power of True Unity
by Ben R. Peters

Available from Kingdom Sending Center
www.kingdomsendingcenter.org

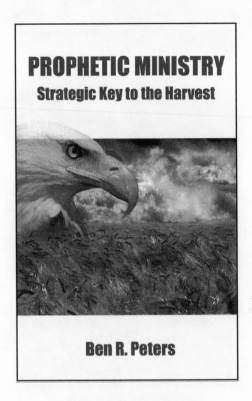

PROPHETIC MINISTRY
Strategic Key to the Harvest

Ben R. Peters

Prophetic Ministry
Strategic Key to the Harvest
by Ben R. Peters

Available from Kingdom Sending Center
www.kingdomsendingcenter.org

Resurrection!
A Manual for Raising the Dead
by Ben R. Peters

Available from Kingdom Sending Center
www.kingdomsendingcenter.org

EXPLORING THE POWER OF THE MIRACULOUS TO BRING PEOPLE TO CHRIST

Signs and Wonders
TO SEEK OR NOT TO SEEK

BEN PETERS
FOREWORD BY BILL HAMON

Signs and Wonders
To Seek or Not to Seek
by Ben R. Peters

Available from Kingdom Sending Center
www.kingdomsendingcenter.org

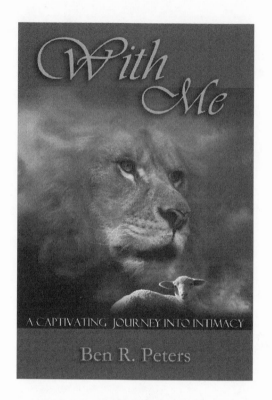

With Me
A Captivating Journey Into Intimacy
by Ben R. Peters

Available from Kingdom Sending Center
www.kingdomsendingcenter.org

Holy Passion: Desire on Fire
Igniting the Torch of Godly Passion
by Ben R. Peters

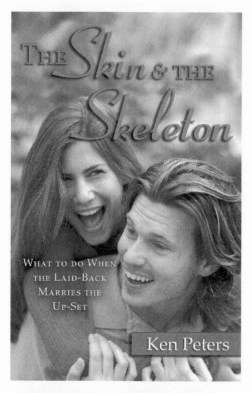

The Skin & the Skeleton
What to Do When the Laid-Back
Marries the Up-Set
by Ken Peters

Available from Kingdom Sending Center
www.kingdomsendingcenter.org

Birthing the Book Within You
Inspiration and Practical Help
to Produce Your Own Book
by Ben R. Peters

Available from Kingdom Sending Center
www.kingdomsendingcenter.org

Made in the USA
Charleston, SC
11 September 2013